Finding

Also by Kathleen Jamie

FINDINGS

ESSAYS ON THE NATURAL AND UNNATURAL WORLD

Kathleen Jamie

Graywolf Press
SAINT PAUL, MINNESOTA

Publication of this volume is made possible in part by a grant provided by
the Minnesota State Arts Board, through an appropriation by the Minnesota
State Legislature; a grant from the Wells Fargo Foundation Minnesota; and
a grant from the National Endowment for the Arts, which believes that a
great nation deserves great art. Significant support has also been provided
by the Bush Foundation; Target; the McKnight Foundation; and other generous contributions from foundations, corporations, and individuals. To these
organizations and individuals we offer our heartfelt thanks.

Published by Graywolf Press
2402 University Avenue, Suite 203
Saint Paul, Minnesota 55114
All rights reserved.

www.graywolfpress.org

Published in the United States of America

ISBN 978-1-55597-445-9

2 4 6 8 9 7 5 3 1
First Graywolf Printing, 2007

Library of Congress Control Number: 2006929506

Cover design: Christa Schoenbrodt, Studio Haus

Cover photograph: Alistair Peebles

Thanks

I met some wonderful people in the course of writing this book; their names are mentioned throughout and to them all I owe a debt of thanks. Some, I'm happy to say, have become friends and they've been kind enough to save me from myself. Mistakes and misapprehensions have been corrected, knowledge generously shared, and my stupidities tactfully brought to my attention before they were set in print.

To Tim Dee, especially for the birds; to Donald Wilkie, skipper of the Annag; to Dawn Kemp, museum curator at the Royal College of Surgeons, Edinburgh; to Sarah Money of the RSPB, to Robin and Caroline Guthrie, Pete Barrass and Don Paterson, many thanks. Colette Bryce shared birds and basking shark enthusiasms, and Krys Hawryszczuk kept hauling me out into the hills, especially during the nappy years.

Things archaeological were explained to me by Steve Watt of Historic Scotland, the staff at Maes Howe, and Dr Simon Gilmour at the Royal Commision on the Ancient and Historical Monuments of Scotland.

Peter Straus and Mary Mount saw the potential in this book from the start. BBC Radio 3 and the editors of the London Review of Books and the Dublin Review were good enough to publish parts en route. Peter Dyer and Henry Iles turned a manuscript into a thing of beauty.

Nat Jansz is a gifted editor: everything was discussed with her, often while walking on Hampstead Heath (those parakeets!). I thank her and Mark Ellingham for their hospitality, commitment and vision.

Finally, I'd like to thank Phil Butler for his continuing gifts of time and space. It was Phil who gave me my first binoculars and encouraged me to buy a mountain bike. To him, and to Duncan and Freya, my love and gratitude.

Contents

Photography Acknowledgments

Photographs by Alistair Peebles © 2007. All rights reserved.

Taken in the following instances with the kind assistance of Historic Scotland (page 2), The Royal College of Surgeons, Edinburgh (page 102), and the Royal Society for the Protection of Birds, Orkney (pages 24, 41, 68).

Alistair Peebles lives and works in Orkney, a group of islands to the north of Scotland where many of these photographs were taken, and the setting for the opening chapter of *Findings*. Born in 1953 and a graduate (in English and Philosophy) of the University of Aberdeen, he combines photography with teaching and writing and spends far too much time in voluntary engagement with the arts. He is nevertheless very glad to be a founding member of the George MacKay Brown Writing Fellowship, established in Orkney in 2006. His most recent exhibition was *Road Works*, with Scottish poet John Glenday.

Findings

Darkness and Light

*They did the deed of darkness
in their own mid-light*

JAMES WRIGHT

Mid-December, the still point of the turning year. It was eight in the morning and Venus was hanging like a wrecker's light above the Black Craig. The hill itself — seen from our kitchen window — was still in silhouette, though the sky was lightening into a pale yellow-grey. It was a weakling light, stealing into the world like a thief through a window someone forgot to close.

The talk was all of Christmas shopping and kids' parties. Quietly, though, like a coded message, an invitation arrived to a meal to celebrate the winter solstice. Only six people would be there, and no electric light.

That afternoon — it was Saturday — we took the kids to the pantomime. This year it was *The Snow Queen.* She was coldly glittery, and swirled around the stage in a platinum cloak with her comic entourage of ravens and spiders. The heroes were a boy and a brave, north-travelling girl. At one point the Snow Queen, in her silver sledge, stormed off stage left, and had she kept going, putting a girdle round the earth, she'd have been following the 56th parallel. Up the Nethergate, out of Dundee, across Scotland, away over the North Atlantic, she'd have made landfall over Labrador, swooped over Hudson's Bay, and have glittered like snowfall somewhere in southern Alaska. Crossing the Bering Sea, then the Sea of Okhotsk, she'd have streaked on through central Moscow, in time, if she really got a move

3

on, to enter stage right for her next line. Of course, we have no realm of snow here, none of the complete Arctic darkness. Nonetheless, when it came time for the Snow Queen to be vanquished for another year, to melt down through a trapdoor leaving only her puddled cloak, everyone was cheered. Before she went, however, the ascendant Sun God kissed the Snow Queen in a quick, knowing, grown-up complicity. I liked that bit.

I like the precise gestures of the sun, at this time of year. When it eventually rises above the hill it shines directly into our small kitchen window. A beam crosses the table and illuminates the hall beyond. In barely an hour, though, the sun sinks again below the hill, south-southeast, leaving a couple of hours of dwindling half-light. Everything we imagine doing, this time of year, we imagine doing in the dark.

I imagined travelling into the dark. Northward — so it got darker as I went. I'd a notion to sail by night, to enter into the dark for the love of its textures and wild intimacy. I had been asking around among literary people, readers of books, for instances of dark as a natural phenomenon, rather than as a cover for all that's wicked, but could find few. It seems to me that our cherished metaphor of darkness is wearing out. The darkness through which might shine the Beacon of Hope. Isaiah's dark: "The people that walked in darkness have seen a great light: they that dwell in the land of the shadow of death, upon them hath the light shined."

Pity the dark: we're so concerned to overcome and banish it, it's crammed full of all that's devilish, like some grim cupboard under the stair. But dark is good. We are conceived and carried in the darkness, are we not? When my son was born, a midwinter child, he cried pitifully at the ward's lights, and only settled to sleep when he was laid in a big pram with a black hood under a black umbrella. Our vocabulary ebbs with the daylight, closes down with the cones of our retinas. I mean, I looked up "darkness" on the Web — and was offered Christian ministries offering to lead me to salvation. And there is always death. We say death is darkness; and darkness death.

In Aberdeen, although it was not yet five o'clock, the harbour lights were lit against the night sky. Ships were berthed right up against the street, and to reach the Orkney and Shetland ferry I had to walk under their massive prows. The ferry *Hrossa* was berthed among other ships, and though the *Hrossa* — the Norse name for Orkney — looked like a toppled office block, and was therefore a ferry, these other vessels were inexplicable mysteries to me, containers of purpose and might. Some carried huge yellow winches, others supported complex and insect-like antennae. The ships were named for strength and warriors, Scots and Norse: the *Highland Patriot,* the *Tor Viking.* I boarded the ferry and went at once out on deck, although it was cold, and leaned over the rail. There was the *Solar Prince* (was it not he who'd kissed the Snow Queen?) and, berthed beside it, the *Edda Frigg.*

The *Edda Frigg* was in the process of putting out. Where she was bound, what her purpose was, I had no idea, but it pleased me that I knew what the name meant: *Edda* — the great Icelandic mythological poems. *Frigg:* Norse goddess, wife of one-eyed Odin. Off she went, the Queen of the Heavens, taking a long moment to pass, first the prow, then the low deck, then the superstructure, stirring the dirty dock water as she went.

Then it was our turn to edge out past other ships. Aberdeen's streetlights, spires and illuminated clock-towers began to recede, and there was the moon itself, above the town. I was shivering now. A sudden flock of seagulls glittered under the harbour lights. Little scenes slipped by: two men hanging on the hook of a crane; stacks of ships' containers; a sudden siren wailing, a line of parked-up lorries; the hammering of metal on metal. We inched past the red-hulled *Viking Crusader,* then the *Hrossa* was out of harbour. At the end of the harbour wall, where it crooks out into the water, stood a humble Christmas tree hung with fairy lights.

Some of the old hands, the Shetland folk for whom the crossing holds no novelty, were already laid flat out on benches. They had a long night ahead; it would take fourteen dark hours before they were in Lerwick for breakfast. Many were students heading home for Christmas. Some were planted in the bar. There was a man with a proper Fair Isle jersey, a girl with a hand-knit tourie. Throughout the whole of the boat — you'd to work hard to find a place to avoid it — Muzak was playing. Christmas hits of yore. Paul McCartney. The only place you could avoid Paul McCartney was a lounge with subdued lighting and big reclining chairs. There were prints on the walls, a set of three, showing a cartoon sea with a stripy lighthouse, a fishing-boat, and below the blue waves, three huge, stupid, cheerful fish. *The Shetland Times*, which a number of the passengers were reading, bore the headline "Day of Reckoning Looms for Fishing."

I'd wanted dark. Real, natural, starry dark, solstice dark, but you can't argue with the moon, and the moon was almost full. It shone through a smir of cloud, spreading its diffused light across the water. The moon had around it an aura of un-colours, the colours of oil spilled on tarmac.

Secretly, I'd been hoping for a moment at sea where there was no human light. Three hundred sixty degrees of winter sea, the only lights those carried by the ship itself. I wanted to be out in the night wind, in wholesome, unbanished darkness. But the *Hrossa* was, after all, only a ferry, and would hug the coast. Nevertheless, I went outside often, to stand shivering on its deck, but there was always a light somewhere. From the port side, small, northern Scottish towns, Brora, perhaps, or Helmsdale, were an orange smudge against the darker line of land. From the starboard side I could look out at the moonlit, fishless sea. Some hours out, I saw three brash lights, in a line to the east, the seaward side. I took them for other vessels, but they were too piled up and intense. They were North Sea oil platforms, and even at this distance they looked frenzied. Maybe this was where the *Solar Prince* and the *Viking Warrior* were bound — on the urgent business of oil. As the ferry drove on, the rigs grew smaller, until they were at the edge of vision, at the edge of the night, as I imagine distant icebergs must look, only on fire.

Then, alone on the metal deck, damp and moonlit, just when I fancied darkness might be complete, I heard a faint call. The boat throbbed on, leaving behind a wave as straight as a glacier. A human call. I must have been mistaken, but listened and — it came again. I scanned the water, there were only the waves, the wide, oil-dark sea. It gave me a fright, and had anyone else been out on deck I might have tugged their arm and said *Listen!* I'm glad I was alone, because, so help me, it was only Elton John. Elton John, piped though a speaker onto the deck. The music was so nearly drowned out by the ship's engines that I'd just caught the top notes. I bent down, stuck my ear next the speaker and, yes, it was Elton John singing, of all things: "Don't let the sun go down on me." I gave up on the dark then, and went below for a drink.

Around midnight, the pilot boat came out to accompany the ferry between the archipelago of low islands into Kirkwall. On all their reefs and hazards, warning lights winked.

~

The Orkney islands, if you don't know them, are green and supine for the most part; a sculptural, wind-honed archipelago. Many of the islands are inhabited. The islands are whale-shapes, as their poet George MacKay Brown has noted. Few trees impede the wind. Water salt and fresh, in wide bays or lochs or channels, is always to hand, lightening and softening the land it encircles. The land is fertile, the people prosperous; Norse and liberal, they live in two main towns and innumerable farms under a huge, energetic sky.

No Orkney weather lasts long, and you can see new weather coming a long way off. There are frequent scraps of rainbow.

And birds. At any point you can stop walking, or pull over and lower the car window and hear the cries of peewits and tremulous curlews. The few inland hills are peat-brown, while at the west, the islands rise to address the Atlantic with fulmar-tenanted cliffs. There is everything you need, except perhaps trees, and more and more people are moving from the south to join the islanders, in search of what they call "a real community." There's that phrase you hear so often: "We fell in love with it."

It had been a long night, and still dark when I woke in the morning. In a hired car, I drove out of Kirkwall toward Finstown, stopping in a layby beside a bottle bank to watch the coming daylight gild the water of the bay. On a stone-built pier a row of oystercatchers was turned to windward. The light was without energy. Above the sleeping shape that was the isle of Shapinsay, the sky mustered a few greys with just a line of creamy yellow. I drove on, out of the village, then turned north over peat-moor. There were cottages by the roadside, bungalows mostly, few nowadays with the traditional flagstone roofs. On Burgar Hill three wind turbines turned sluggishly and a ragged skein of geese flew above them. The islands have been farmed for a very long time, and if you climb a hill and look down onto the green lands below, the farmhouses are so plentiful they look as though they've been shaken out from a box.

Six hours of daylight, a meagre ration. I'd an appointment at sunset, about three o'clock, so there was time for a spot of birdwatching, and a walk on the cliffs. I drove down straight tracks between farms and wire fences, left the car in a layby at the shore, and walked up onto the headland called Marwick Head. On the sea below the cliffs a lobster boat hung with pink buoys bounced through the water. The westerly wind brought squalls in like grey wings. Only a few fulmars were at home, the puffins' burrows were empty, waiting for spring. A pair of ravens, Odin's birds, seemed to follow me along the clifftop, making comments to each other in their lovely intimate cronking. Underfoot were brown and brittle dry sea pinks.

Last night I'd wanted dark, but was frustrated. Now, conversely, it was clear light I was hoping for. I was going to Maes Howe, and if the visit was to be effective the southern sky had to be clear of cloud, at least for a few crucial moments at sunset. I walked on the cliffs at Marwick Head, keeping a weather eye on the banks of cloud that filled the southern sky. Now and again a shaft of light broke through, illuminating the land below. Headlands jutted out into the sea, each behind the last. Some are tremendously high. St John's Head, on Hoy, falls 1,300 feet to the sea. I could just see the famous stack called the Old Man of Hoy standing proud of the cliffs behind. Then, farther, the few isolated mountains of the Scottish mainland appeared to float on a pool of citrine light.

I like the sun's particular gestures, and I like the signs of midwinter life: the wintering geese in empty fields, a lone woman walking along a farm track in boots and coat, a scarf over her head.

A drive, a spot of birdwatching, a sandwich and a walk on the cliffs, and by half-past two what daylight had been grudgingly dealt out was being gathered in again. The distant hills were black and bulky. When I got back to the car, the sun was so low it was shining directly through the windscreen, dazzling bright, and this was a good sign. As I drove, the empty winter fields revealed a secret presence of water, in dips and reed-beds, orange-coloured and aglow like precious things. I even saw a hen harrier, gliding above some rust-tipped reeds at a lochside, its wings held in the shallowest of Vs. The dead of winter, so called.

I have a friend who is both a poet and a church-goer and I was grumbling to him about the redundant metaphor of Darkness and Light. I was saying that the dark, the natural, courteous dark, was too much maligned and, frankly, I blamed Christians. The whole idea wanted refreshing. We couldn't see the real dark for the metaphorical dark. Because of the metaphorical dark, the death dark, we were constantly concerned to banish the natural dark. Enough of this "Don't let the sun go down on me" stuff. I told my friend I wanted to go into the dark, that I'd a notion to visit Maes Howe at solstice. At that he raised an eyebrow. "Maes Howe?" he said. "But Maes Howe *is* a metaphor, isn't it?"

The building nowadays known as Maes Howe is a Neolithic chambered cairn, a tomb where, 5,000 years ago, they interred the bones of the dead. In its long, long existence it has been more forgotten about than known, but in our era it is open to the public, with tickets and guides and explanatory booklets. It stands, a mere grassy hump in a field, in the central plain of Mainland Orkney. There is a startling collection of other Neolithic sites nearby.

To reach Maes Howe I took the road that passes over a thin isthmus between two lochs. On the west side is a huge brooding stone circle, the Ring of Brodgar. On the east, like three elegant women conversing at a cocktail party, are the Standing Stones of Stenness. The purpose of these may be mysterious, but a short seven miles away is the Neolithic village called Skara Brae. There is preserved a huddle of roofless huts, dug half underground into midden and sand dune. There, you can marvel at the domestic normality, that late Stone Age people had beds and cupboards and neighbours and beads. You can feel both their presence, their day-to-day lives, and their utter absence. It's a good place to go. It re-calibrates your sense of time.

Two men were standing at the car park at Maes Howe car park. The taller, older man was wearing a white shirt and improbable tartan trousers. As I stepped out of the car, he shook his head sadly. The younger man was dressed for outdoors, somewhat like a traffic warden, with a woollen hat pulled down to his eyes and a navy-blue coat. For a moment we all looked at each other. The taller man spoke first.

"Not looking good, I'm afraid."

The timing was right, the sun was setting, but . . .

"Cloud," said the tall man.

"Can't be helped," I replied.

"Will you go in, anyway? You can't always tell, you just need a moment when the cloud breaks . . ."

Alan, an Englishman in Historic Scotland tartan trousers, led me into a little shop to issue a ticket. The shop was housed in an old water mill, some distance from the tomb, and sold guidebooks and fridge magnets and tea towels. From the window you could see over the main road to the tomb.

"Tell you what," he said. "I'll give you a ticket so you can come back tomorrow, if you like, but I can't give you one for the actual solstice, Saturday. We start selling them at two-thirty on the actual solstice. It's first come, first served."

"How many people come?"

"Well, we can accommodate twenty-five, at a pinch."

But today there was only myself.

The young guide, Rob, was waiting outside. A workman's van hurtled past, then we crossed the road, entered through a wicket gate and followed a path across the field. We were walking toward the tomb by an indirect route that respected the wide ditch around the site. Sheep were grazing the field, and a heron was standing with its aristocratic back to us. There was a breeze, and the shivery call of a curlew descending. On all sides there are low hills, holding the plain between them. To the south, the skyline is dominated by two much bigger, more distant hills, a peak and a plateau. Though you wouldn't know it from here, they belong to another island, to Hoy. Above these dark hills, in horizontal bars, were the offending clouds.

You enter into the inner chamber of the tomb by a low passageway more than twenty-five feet long. It's more of a journey than a gateway. You don't have to crawl on hands and knees, but neither can you walk upright. The stone roof bears down on your spine; a single enormous slab of stone forms the wall you brush with your left shoulder. You must walk in that stooped position just a moment too long, so when you're admitted to the cairn two sensations come at once: you're glad to stand, and the other is a sudden appreciation of stone. You are admitted into a solemn place which is not a heart at all, or even a womb, but a cranium.

You are standing in a high, dim stone vault. There is a thick soundlessness, like a recording studio, or a strongroom. A moment ago, you were in the middle of a field, with the wind and curlews calling. That world has been taken away, and the world you have entered into is not like a cave, but a place of artifice, of skill. Yes, that's it, what you notice when you stand and look around is cool, dry, applied skill. Across five thousand years you can still feel their self-assurance.

The walls are of red sandstone, dressed into long rectangles, with a tall sentry-like buttress in each corner to support the corbelled roof. The passage to the outside world is at the base of one wall. Set waist-high into the other three are square openings into cells which disappear into the thickness of the walls. That's where they laid the dead, once the bones had been cleaned of flesh by weather and birds. The stone blocks which would once have sealed these graves lie on the gravel floor. And the point is, the ancients who built this tomb orientated it precicely: the long passageway faces exactly the setting midwinter sun. Consequently, for the few days around the winter solstice a beam of the setting sun shines along the passage, and onto the tomb's back wall. In recent years, people have crept along the passageway at midwinter to witness this, the complicit kiss. Some, apparently, find it overwhelming.

We crossed the field. The heron took to the air. I dawdled behind. My guide, the young Rob, was waiting at the entrance, which is just a low square opening at the bottom of the mound. I glanced back at the outside world, the road, the clouded sky over Hoy's hills, which did not look promising; then we crept inside and for a long minute walked doubled over, until Rob stood and I followed.

Inside was bright as a tube train, and the effect was brutal. I'd expected not utter darkness, but perhaps a wombish-red. Rob was carrying a torch but this light revealed every crack, every joint and fissure in the ancient stonework. At once a man's voice said, "Sorry, I'll switch it off," but the moment was lost and, any-way, I'd been forewarned. As he sold me the ticket, Alan had told me that surveyors were inside the cairn, with all their equip-ment. "A bit of a problem," was how he'd put it. And here they were. We entered the tomb and, in that fierce white light, it was like that moment which can occur in midlife, when you look at your mother and realise with a shock that she is old.

The surveyers, commissioned by Historic Scotland, were doing a project that involved laser-scanning, photogrammetry, and pulse-radar inspection. They were working inside the tomb, and had been for days. A huge implement, I couldn't tell if it was a torch or a camera, lay on a schoolroom chair. There was a telephone in one of the grave-cells. There were two surveyors. One was folded, foetus-like, into the little cell in the back wall. I could see only his legs. He grunted as he shifted position.

"Strange place to spend your working day," I remarked.

"You're not wrong," he replied, sourly.

His older colleague seemed glad for a break. He stood, a portly man in a black tracksuit and fleece jacket, and stretched his back. Somehow he dimmed the light and the tomb settled back into restful gloom. The outside world was a square at the far end of the long passageway. There would be no sunset.

"Too bad," the surveyor said. "Oh, well."

Rob, hunched in his woolly hat, drew breath and raised his torch as though to begin the guided tour, but he paused.

"Been here before?" he asked me.

"Several times."

He said, "We're on the Web now, y'know," and gestured with the torch to a camera mounted on the Neolithic wall. "Live. Don't go picking your nose."

"Watch your eyes!" said the voice from the grave-chamber, then came a detonating flash.

The tomb had fallen into disuse. Four thousand winters passed, four thousand solstices. Then a party of Vikings arrived en route to the Crusades. They broke into the tomb to take refuge from a storm, and probably cleared out what they found inside: bones, backfill. The Vikings passed the tedious hour by hatching names and witticisms on the stones — Maes Howe contains the best collection of Runic inscriptions outwith Iceland. "Crusaders broke into this howe," they say. "Many a woman has walked stooping in here."

The Vikings went away, leaving many messages, but Maes Howe was again half-forgotten, a fairy place, a strange mound on a heath. Generations lived and died. We invented electric light, the internal combustion engine, we exploited oilfields, developed telephones and TVs, to dispel the winter dark — and now at solstice we come, as no one has done for nigh on five thousand years, to witness a little beam of sunlight creeping through the darkness onto a stone wall.

The surveyors had been beset by technical problems. They were behind schedule and fed up. The younger man unfolded himself from the grave-cell, and I asked him what it was he was doing. "Just stereo photography," he said. "Pass me that light meter, would you?" He folded himself back into the grave.

Stereo photography works on the same principle as our own eyes and, like our eyes, gives us a 3D image. With the right computer equipment, they would generate a complete 3D image of the interior of the tomb, which you could look at on a screen. It would be an accurate, absolutely precise record of what it's like in there. The work had been commissioned because Historic Scotland, who are charged with care of the monument, are anxious to know if the building is moving. There are tiny fissures and cracks in the stonework — that brash light revealed them all. They might have happened in time out of mind, when the building was new. On the other hand, the tiny cracks might be more recent, which would be worrying. The surveyors would make their images, and then in eighteen months come back and do it all again, and then, by comparing the two results, they would discern the slightest difference, the slightest shift in the structure. Rob was explaining it to me. "There's other problems too," he said. "Look." He pointed out a green smear on a high stone. "Algae."

Many visitors come crawling along the entrance tunnel to marvel at the tomb, and they breathe. The building wasn't designed to be breathed in and lit. It was designed to be dead in, and dark. Breath and light mean algae, and algae is damaging. A tiny humidity recorder had been installed to monitor the levels of moisture within the tomb.

Further, there was the roof above our heads. It was not original, but the work of enthusiastic Victorian archaeologists. They had awakened Maes Howe out of a long sleep, by entering through its roof, as you might crack a boiled egg. Though they had repaired their damage, it was not to the Neolithic standard, and a watchful eye was being kept on it. And there was more. When it was constructed, the tomb had been clad in waterproof clay before being covered in a thick layer of earth and turf — the prehistoric builders knew what they were doing — but the waterproofing had since been punctured. These damages, too, could admit insidious, creeping moisture. Though it was known the waterproofing had been damaged, no one could tell exactly where. Rather than scalp all the earth from the monument to investigate, they were doing it the modern way: a pulse-radar survey. And then there were the carvings. Broaches in the layer of waterproof clay might admit not only damp, but tiny scouring particles of the clay itself. The worry was that, as these particles washed slowly into the interior and migrated down the stonework, they may slowly be wearing away the carvings there. Rob lit with his torch Maes Howe's famous little lion, which is a delicate carving about the size of your fist, etched on a tall slab.

That was Viking work, but the tomb also contains Neolithic carvings: strange, nervy conjoined triangle and diamond shapes.

As Rob shone his torch on the little lion, instinctively I lifted my hand to touch it, to make a gesture of connection.

"Please don't," he said.

That's why we are minded by a guide. Too many wandering, sweaty fingers would soon wear the carvings away.

"Well," Rob said. "We don't know for sure if they are wearing away. That's what these surveyors are here to find out. Laser-scanning. If they made a laser scan of each surface, and then repeat it in eighteen months, they'd be able to tell, because the lasers can measure loss of thousandth of a millimetre . . ."

Rob shoved his torch in his pocket. "You see it's a World Heritage Site now," he said. "You can't mess with a World Heritage Site. But it's not doing too badly. I mean, how many other five-thousand-year-old buildings do you know?"

"Last longer than a Wimpey house," said a voice from the cell at the back.

"So that's why they're taking all these measurements. And who'll pay for it? The taxpayer. That's who. The taxpayer."

The younger man worked on, but the elder of the surveyors joined Rob and me, and in the sombre hush of the tomb we talked. Polite strangers, we stood with our hands on our hips, regarding this consummate Neolithic stonework, this ancient house of the dead, this metaphor, and talked about property prices. I can't remember if we spoke in low voices, as you would in a sacred place. I think we must have, because you could sense the stern weight of stone and earth overhead.

Nothing's certain in this life but death and taxes. I'd been thwarted last night, leaning on the deck-rail, in my hope of sailing into real northern dark, and disappointed again this short midwinter day that no beam of sunlight would enter the tomb. But something interesting was happening here. It occured to me, sometime during our brief conversation, that I would never again get so close to real Neolithic ancestors. Had this scene not happened before, thousands of years ago? Had not skilled workmen stood within this very tomb at the end of a working day, and taken a moment to survey their handiwork? Real people, flesh on their bones, tools in their hands, words on their lips in some language now utterly lost? I glanced behind me. The young surveyor was sitting hunched in the cell, his knees bent up. He sighed, and passed his weary hand over his face.

We spoke about the recent fire in Edinburgh, which had destroyed some buildings in the Old Town, and wondered if they could be rebuilt. Could we ever afford to rebuild them? The surveyor, as befitted his profession, asked if anyone actually knew what they looked like. Had they photographs? Drawings? Measurements? I remarked that they'd rebuilt parts of bombed-out Warsaw using the paintings of Canaletto's nephew, Bernardo Bellotto.

"You could build a replica of this, now," said Rob. No, seriously, with all this data you could build an exact replica of Maes Howe. . . ."

"What, in the field next door?"

He shrugged. "It's not impossible, you know."

Rob stayed behind with the surveyors while I made the smallest and most changing of journeys, squeezing down a passageway and out into the world of sound and moving air. Dry winter grasses nodded in the breeze. By then, the sun had well and truly gone down on me, the clouds in the southern sky were glowing ruby-red above the hills. There had been no starry dark, and no sunset play of light. Oh well. I crossed the field and then the road, and back at the shop Alan, in his Historic Scotland tartan breeks, stood behind his counter. We drank coffee from a machine, and had a conversation about technology, about how the interior of a Neolithic tomb could be seen on a website. Then, as it happened, the phone rang. It was a local man telling Alan the website had a glitch, that he'd have to unplug everything and plug it all in again. The southwestern clouds were deep garnet-coloured now. Alan called into the tomb on the phone, asked Rob to fiddle with the webcam, then hung up.

"Technology, eh?" He shook his head. "Shall I show you what we do when it all breaks down?"

He left his post behind the desk and crossed the shop, picking up from a wicker basket two Frisbees, one red, one blue. "If I hold them up in that window there, I can send a signal to Rob. Red Frisbee means 'Stay over at the tomb, more visitors are coming.' Blue means 'You can come back now.'"

It was almost dark when I went back down to the car and, when I did the two surveyors were emerging from the tomb to go for their tea. They were figures crossing a darkening field, with the mound of Maes Howe behind them. One of them lifted his hand high in salutation, and I waved back, and for a moment they looked like astronauts emerging from a capsule after a successful mission.

That's what we'd been talking about, Alan and me. What, if the world lasts, would people five thousand years hence find worth saving of our age? They could scarce avoid all our plastic and junk, but what would they want? Something at the top of our competence, something that expressed the drama of our times and beliefs. Is there anything they'd come from afar to see, and find almost overwhelming? But, Alan said, there would be no need to keep anything, no need to come from afar. It would all be on virtual reality. Like now, with all this stereo photography and laser-scanning and photogrammetry and what have you, you could switch on your computer at home, put on your goggles and walk stooping into Maes Howe.

I got into the car, turned the ignition, switched on the lights. The Apollo moon landing gear, that's what. Those contraptions like washing machines wrapped in tin foil that were launched into lightless space, sometime in the Oil Age. That's what we should keep. And maybe an offshore rig, where men actually worked day and night, slathered in the stuff, that we could have heat and movement and light. Let the future marvel over that. I pulled out onto the road, and drove to Stromness.

In Stromness' narrow, eighteenth-century street, it was time for coffee and cake and some Christmas shopping. I wandered into a toy shop, all bright and lit for Christmas, and in there picked up a silver plastic tiara. My little daughter had liked the Snow Queen; she would love this. Standing there in the bright shop with this ridiculous tiara in my hand, turning it so it sparkled, I was thinking about light. I suppose I'd been hoping for a trick of the light at Maes Howe. No, trick was the wrong word. The tomb-builders had constructed their cairn to admit a single beam of solstice light: it was the bending of a natural phenomenon to a human end, somewhere between technology and art. But not art either: drama. "Nowhere," said George MacKay Brown, "is the drama of dark and light played out more starkly than in the north." A very ancient drama, going right back to the Neolithic. Were they the first people, I wondered, to articulate this metaphor of light and dark, of life and death. . . .

Then the shop-keeper said "enjoy it while it lasts."

"I'm sorry?"

She nodded toward the plastic tiara in my hand.

"My little girl used to love these things, all glittery and bright. But she's fourteen now, and wears nothing but black."

———

The surveyors finished their task very late that night, apparently, and were gone on the morning ferry, leaving the tomb ready for its little crowd of solstice visitors. I amost envied the surveyors the chance to move and work in the thick silence of the chambered cairn, passing laser beams over its stones. Few people can have spent so long within its confines since it was built. You pass a light-beam over the stone and record the infinitesimal time it takes to return to source. Light's echo. Time at the speed of light.

My ventures into light and dark had been ill-starred. I'd had no dramatic dark, neither at sea nor in the tomb, and no resurrecting beam of sunlight. But lasers are light, aren't they? Intensified, organised light. I'd crept into Maes Howe at solstice, hoping for Neolithic technology; what I'd found was the technology of the twenty-first century. Here were skilled people passing light over these same stones, still making meaurements by light and time. That thought pleased me.

———

For five thousand years we have used darkness as the metaphor of our mortality. We were at the mercy of merciless death, which is darkness. When we died, they sent a beam of midwinter light in among our bones. What a tender, potent gesture. In the Christian era, we were laid in our graves to face the rising sun. We're still mortal, still don't want to die, don't want our loved ones to die. That's why the surveyors waved so heartily — if I'd spent ten days working in the house of the dead, dammit, I'd come out waving, too.

We have not banished death, but we have banished the dark. We have light, we have oilfields and electricity and lasers. And by the light we have made, we can see that there are, metaphorically speaking, cracks. We are doing damage, and have a growing sense of responsibility. The surveyors poring over the tomb are working in an anxious age. We look about the world, by the light we have made, and realise it's all vulnerable, and all worth saving, and no one can do it but us.

And, if it all goes to hell on a handcart, we have the data, we can build a replica. Maybe five thousand years from now we will indeed be living among replicas. We may be replicas ourselves. It's not impossible. But I have my doubts.

———

I could have waited a couple of days and then joined that little group squeezing into the tomb at the solstice proper. But I had my own midwinter rituals to observe. We put up the Christmas tree on the 21st, the children decorate it, and I couldn't miss that. There was the dinner with friends to look forward to as well. I would leave the next day.

There was time, nonetheless, for an evening walk. Of course it was dark; it had been for hours. The houses at the edge of town were lit, and their curtains drawn. Beyond the houses, beyond the reach of the yellow streetlights, there is the golf course. The golf course! Shorn and mellow by day, in the dark it reverted to the wild. Its gentle mounds and slopes seemed almost to breathe, to edge more closely than they do by daylight. A narrow road bound by a stone wall and a ditch bisected it. There were unseen ruts to negotiate.

Where the road ended at the shore there was a large fishermen's hut with lobster creels stacked on its lee side, and beyond that — the sea. Not the open sea, but a fierce channel between two islands. I huddled against the hut, sheltering from the wind. Out in the night was the low, shapely isle of Graemsay, with lighthouses at either end, and behind it the cliffs of Hoy rose to their full 1,300 feet. Vast tonnages of water fight through a narrow channel here, to flood or drain the great natural anchorage of Scapa Flow. The surging sea, the wind, the cliffs' bulk against the night sky were (forgive me) sublime. There was much sound: wind, and waves, but also a silent light show: the beams of many lighthouses shone and faded shyly across the water, each to its own pulse. The pathways they made on the black surface of the sea slipped in and out of existence. Here were all the textures of darkness — bulwarks of land, shifting sea, dark starry sky, and the consolation of lighthouses. And in the distance, among further dark islands, rose the flare-stack of the Flotta oil refinery. Oil is brought there from the North Sea fields by tanker or pipeline, and by day and night excess gas is burned off into the atmosphere, in an orange flame.

Nowadays, though, they're experimenting with tide-power, with setting turbines right here in the tidal race between these islands. The hope is that the sea can generate a constant power, a contant heat and light which will be renewable and unpolluting. That's the idea. Wind turbines are fine, but sometimes the wind drops. There's the sun, but, as we know, sometimes it's obscured by clouds. Tides and the moon, however, you can rely on.

I don't know if the twenty-five or so people who crept into Maes Howe for the solstice were rewarded with a beam of sunlight. And if it came, did they part to let it through, like a doctor at an accident? I was at home again by then, and we were going out for dinner.

The hallway of our friends' cottage was inviting in candle-light, as was the room, and the table. The curtains were open to show black night pressed against the windows. We were a merry company, and in the warm candlelight we enjoyed a half-joking, symbolic meal. We ate stuffed red peppers, to symbol-ise, our host said, the rising sun. Sautéed carrot sticks were its warming rays, and green beans, presented with a flourish, rep-resented the shoots of spring. We cheered the beans, and drank a toast, because tonight was midwinter's night, the night of the complicit kiss, and tomorrow the light would begin its return.

DATE		SIGHTINGS	NAME
4/6	CALM	WREN, ♂ PHEASANT	
		B-H GULL, HEN HARRIER	
15/6		♂ + ♀, RABBIT	
		H. Harrier ♂, S.E. Owl	
16.6		Blue Hare	
18.6		4pm H. Harrier ♂	
4.00		Curlew	
		Oystercatcher	
		Meadow Pipit	
		Stonechat ♂ + ♀	
		Hooded Crows	
		Redshank.	
		Kestrel	
		Hen Harrier ♀ — Hunting close	23/6
		Pheasant (Heard) to hide	
		Hen Harrier ♂ —	
		Pied Wagtail	

Peregrines, Ospreys, Cranes

She has been calling for this week and last — the first half of a dry April. The sound enters my attic room through its window, and if I turn from my desk to glance out of that window I see the hill. She has been calling from up there.

Our narrow garden and the neighbours' gardens run up toward that hill. I say gardens but properly speaking they're orchards, and the plum and pear trees are coming into blossom. A couple of doors along they keep hens and the cockerel crows all day. I hear him, but also I hear the peregrine's thin shriek, over and over, like a turnstile pleading for oil.

Peregrine falcons are rare birds which do not breed in these parts. But they are here. I can see them, and the entire town, if it's a mind to listen, can hear her cry. It's the kind of sound that drills into your head, and even when she's silent you carry the sound in your brain. The ledge the birds have chosen is seventy feet or so up on a north-facing cliff. Parts of the cliff are unstable and prone to landslip. At its base is an undergrowth of brambles; at the top thin birches, hawthorns, and the wild cherries known in Scotland as gean. Above that, the land slopes back and rises steeply into a hill.

I watched her yesterday. She was upright on the edge of her favoured ledge with her back to the world, the long brown wings folded down to her tail. She was calling and calling. People are beginning to talk — is that a bird? A lost lamb? Someone said he thought it was an injured animal at a roadside, a hare or fox. But, though half the town can hear it, the male peregrine must know this sound is intended for him alone. How it must nail through his brain. You. You. He was perched on a lichen-spotted lip of rock some feet away, and had also turned his back. She is bigger, and more brown. His back was the colour of slate roofs after rain. What you see when they swivel their heads round is the white of their cheeks.

As she called and called, he stood like a child in a huff. Then he opened his wings and fell into the air. He flew in an easy loop, and when the sunlight glanced his undersides they were pale and banded like rippled sycamore. He swooped round, then arrived back and landed on the female. Their mating lasted a few brief seconds; there was a fluster of wings and it looked as though they might overbalance, but then he fell away into space and made a wide loop again before settling on his own ledge. But she was sated only for a moment, then she started again. You. You.

So there we are. Nesting peregrines. Another damn thing to worry about.

In some places, peregrines' nests are guarded round the clock for fear of egg-snatchers or unscrupulous falconers who'd take the young. Ospreys, the big fisher-birds, are vulnerable to egg thieves too. I learned about our local ospreys' nest from a certain old man, whom I often meet if I'm out cycling. A round-faced fellow in his seventies, on fine days he walks the hills and byways behind the town. I don't know his name. He carries a small pair of binoculars and we always have the same conversation.

I stop the bike and brightly enquire, "Anything interesting?" He's generous with his observations and will tell me about buzzards or butterflies. Then we say, where is everyone? There are 2,500 people in this town, but even on a glorious day we have the hills and woods to ourselves. "Ach — the young wans are no interestit," he'll say, shaking his head. His own concern is almost Jainish. Once he was annoyed that horse-riders had allowed their animals to gallop through a certain puddle, scattering the water with no heed for the pond-skaters there. No thought for the insects at all.

To see the ospreys I cycled to the vantage point the old man had described. There was a view downhill and across green fields to the estuary. At the riverside was a stand of trees with a Scots pine among them, and sure enough I could see through binoculars that the pine sported a ridiculous toupee made of sticks. Furthermore, there was a bird standing upright on top of it, like a glove puppet, surveying the river. Had the old man not told me, I'd never have noticed it, but now it was obvious.

That was last year, and now spring had come again I resolved to take my first chance to see if these big birds had safely made the journey north.

The rockface remained in shade till afternoon. The male peregrine was there today, sitting side-on, glumly inspecting his feet. He lifted first one yellow talon then the other, like one who has chewing gum on his shoe. His breast is creamy and it showed up in contrast to the rock and his grey back. Then he settled himself, facing outward to the view, and although he seemed at rest his head kept moving. Terribly, lecherously, his eye fell on every passing bird. He checked the sky constantly. In a single minute, he shifted his gaze twenty times, left, right, directly overhead, more often than a Formula One driver changes gear. There's a line I think of whenever I glimpse a bird of prey on a fence post, or watch a kestrel hovering. If you've seen the hawk, be sure, the hawk has seen you.

Everyone's saying this weather can't last. "We'll pay for it!" we agree, in our gleeful Calvinism. Fancy — day after day of summer sunshine, in April. The house grows dusty and neglected because we spend so much time outdoors. It's unseasonal, but all weather is unseasonal nowadays. The plum blossom is coming and next door's old pear tree is a perfect triangle of greenish-white froth. They do this like a conjuring trick, the old trees. They're brittle and cronish all winter, then blossom issues out of them and fills the tree slowly, like a dancehall filling on a Saturday night.

The peregrines have no interest in plum blossom and buds. They leave that to the bullfinches and blue tits. There are other tenants of the cliff, jackdaws mostly, and some wood pigeons. The jackdaws sit side by side, like pairs of shoes, on their various niches. I wonder if they're unnerved by their neighbours. Where the jackdaws are cosy and domestic in their arrangements, the peregrines stand upright at a distance to each other, but linked with the heightened tension, almost, of flamenco dancers. That's it — the peregrines have *duende.*

I saw the male about 7 p.m. from my window. He was flying with quick wings. The swept-back, tapering wings whip faster than you'd imagine, with a quick flicking or rowing motion. He had something clutched in his feet. It was a small blackness, concussed or already dead. He flew not to his ledge but away up onto the hill, to eat in peace.

The town's jackdaws all rise at once, swirl over the gardens clucking before they land again on the trees and rock ledges. The peregrines are all vista — their high ledge affords them a view of the entire estuary, from the mountains almost to the sea, in all its greys and blues, its reeds and its river islands. A view, if indeed they see "views" at all, of water and air. At ebb-tide, the estuary's exposed sandbanks are long wing-shapes crowded with feeding birds. Immediately below the peregrines, however, are the pitched slate roofs of the town, and its many disused chimneys. Chimneys are the jackdaws' haunt, and I envy them their elevated life, at once part of a household and part of the wide air.

As April passed, I looked up books and field guides, because I knew nothing about peregrines. Do they mate and then build a nest, or vice versa? Some birds of prey mate many, many times. Ospreys, apparently, do it hundreds of times before the eggs are laid. I don't know if peregrines construct a nest at all, or if they just deposit eggs on the rock ledge, like sea birds do. These are new questions to me. When I want to know a thing, I resort to books and feel strangely exposed without books to fall back on, as though standing on a ledge. I must just learn to be patient, learn to observe first-hand.

As they have their persecutors, their poisoners and egg thieves, birds of prey have their allies too. It's like life during wartime: you don't know whom you can trust. The best view of the nest site can be had from a garage, and I was hanging about there today, trying to look nonchalant, trying to raise the binoculars without being obvious, but the mechanic appeared whistling from his workshop and caught me in the act.

"Looking for the peregrines?" he asked. "Boy, she was making a racket this morning."

He glanced over his shoulder, but his boss was busy in his office and so the mechanic beckoned me to follow him. He had a rolling gait, his hands thrust in the pockets of his blue overalls, a mobile phone clipped to his belt. He was walking toward a dirty oil-drum. When we got there, he lifted aside an old coat. It was concealing from his boss a telescope mounted on a low stand.

"Take a look," he said. "Handsome birds. Aye, I'm keeping an eye on them."

~

There is a book, and late the other night, when the kids were asleep and the birds at roost, I made a tour through the Internet's second-hand bookstores, and this morning the postman brought my purchase: J.A. Baker's *The Peregrine.* Published in 1967, this is a classic of English natural history; a keen, affecting book about a man's affiliation with his countryside and these particular birds. It's out of print now, and my copy had travelled up country from Bristol. Written on the flyleaf is the name of the previous owner, John Hunter, which sounds like a folk name for the peregrine himself.

~

The hot days continued, but began each morning with a thick damp haar, which smells of the sea, twenty miles away. Early in the morning I watched the female peregrine fly through the mist on whirring wings. She was carrying the carcass of a kill into the recess of her ledge. In the afternoon, when the mist had burned off and the day became hot, I took the book outside, intending to begin it. It was the school holidays, and our children and next door's were playing in the garden. I settled to read and at once learned that the peregrine's eyes are bigger and heavier than our own.

Suddenly a formation of fighter jets sheared overhead. I wanted to cover my ears, but made myself keep listening, to hear what the birds did. My son came running up to me, then came another outrage of noise: three more jets tearing through the pale sky. My son is seven, he wanted to jump in excitement, he wanted to run indoors and draw fighter-planes.

Later, the radio said that RAF Leuchars had "welcomed home" its Tornadoes from Iraq. Those must have been the very planes that had screamed over our garden, in formation, home from the faraway war we had watched on TV. The jets' terrible noise had obliterated all else, but the garden birds took up their twitterings at once, greenfinches in the plum trees.

I looked for the peregrines later, but they were not there. J.A. Baker writes, "The peregrine lives in a pouring-away world of no attachment, a world of wakes and tilting, of sinking planes of land and water." I could envy that, sometimes. Later still, my son asked if we were to be bombed. "No," I said. "We will not be bombed."

Peregrine falcons kill their prey by diving down on it from above. They have other methods, but this dive, called a stoop, is the most spectacular. They can gain a lot of height, fold their wings and fall through the air at anything up to 150 miles an hour, with a howling sound. The victim, snatched in flight by this terror from above, probably knows nothing. It is knocked cold by the impact, and then killed by a bite through the neck from the hawk's hooked beak. Though I scan the sky, I have never seen the peregrines hunt. Once, though, I saw the female step off her ledge and drop like a stone into an elder tree forty feet below. The tree exploded with jackdaws.

By Easter Sunday, the run of hot weather had broken. A bitter east wind blew from the sea. As is the custom, we hard-boiled some eggs and the youngsters painted them, and we went to the park to roll the eggs downhill. Few people were there, though, and we soon dispersed. I saw the male peregrine in the afternoon being pursued round the cliff by a single crow. The crow veered off and went to sit in a tree, but it must have left the peregrine piqued, because he circled alone two or three times more, stooping as though in scorn at whatever happened to be flying beneath him. A jackdaw jinked away with its life. Then the peregrine flew up and away over the hill, and was silhouetted for a long moment against the misty sunlight. An hour later he was back. On another ledge, six feet below, was what looked like a burst cushion, pigeon-pink-grey.

"We'll pay for it" — and now how it rains. Streams run in the gutters and top-soil off the fields. The female falcon was hunched under an overhang, with her back turned like a cartoon dunce in a classroom corner, but no dunce she. You could tell she was alert, her head swivelled at every movement. The low cloud brought an almost pleasing melancholia. I walked on the hill. Lambs were sheltering under an old hawthorn. But after the rain, two full days of it, came a day so bright and washed clean, everything was rinsed: the sky and trees, gutters and windows, even the splashes of bird lime below the peregrines' ledge were washed away. In the clear air the male falcon himself looked sharper, his grey back was sleek, his beak and talons buttercup-bright.

J.A. Baker says peregrines bathe every day in fresh running streams. He spent ten years concerning himself with peregrines in East Anglia, spending whole days roaming the countryside, hiding in ditches, cycling along lanes, examining the carcasses of birds the peregrines had killed to eat. There is not a bird he doesn't know and cannot evoke. Myself, I keep the binoculars about me, and catch a glance at coffee-time, or before fetching the children from school. Where would I look, if I wanted to find the birds in their peregrinations? Where the falcon hunts or bathes, I have no idea.

I have no idea either about J.A. Baker, not even his Christian name. He has utterly effaced himself from his book. The book carried the dedication "to my wife" — that is the only clue to his life. But there is almost a tradition in literature of lone men engaging with birds. T.H. White, in his strange memoir of his retreat into falconry, *The Goshawk,* alludes only to his fear of approaching war; there is Paul Gallico's affecting *Snow Goose.* Think of *The Bird Man of Alcatraz.* As it happens, our local theatre is staging *Kes,* and there are posters in shop windows which show a boy gazing up at the falcon as it hovers with its tail fanned against an azure sky. Even a book so recent as William Fiennes's *The Snow Geese* is a convalescent's journey.

Between the laundry and the fetching kids from school, that's how birds enter my life. I listen. During a lull in the traffic, oyster catchers. In the school playground, sparrows — what few sparrows are left — chirp from the eaves. There are old swallows' nests up there. It's late April, but where are the swallows? The birds live at the edge of my life. That's okay. I like the sense that the margins of my life are semi-permeable. Where the peregrines go when they're not at their rock ledge, I couldn't say.

By the last days of April the swallows had arrived to twitter on our telephone wire. I refocused, and there were the peregrines sitting a yard apart up on the cliff. He was still as stone, like a little votive statue on a high plinth. She was restless, stretching and preening. She lifted her wing and stretched it slantwise across her back, a balletic movement. Then she scratched her ear with her yellow claw. Then she preened her breast. It was about 8:30 on a Saturday morning. The children came into my room demanding breakfast, but I was leaning out of the window in my nightclothes staring through binoculars. I thought she might be going to fly soon, and wanted to catch the exact moment when she stepped off the ledge and flew, to see where she headed.

"Swallows are back. Can you hear them?" I said.

"Mum, can we have our breakfast?"

"Just a minute . . ."

Dammit. I'd glanced away for a moment, and when I looked back the peregrine had quit fidgeting and flown. But the door burst open again. "Mum — can we have our breakfast? In the living room? So we can watch the cartoons on telly?"

"Yes," I said. " I'm coming."

I took an hour at lunchtime to cycle out and see if the ospreys were on the nest, this year as last, and they were. Even from two fields away I could see a black and white head, like a helmeted guard looking over a rampart. There was a stiff breeze and blousy clouds; the light was so bright it made your eyes ache. The tide was in and I made my way down to the estuary by a farm track which ended at a place where a smaller river empties into the Firth. When it got too muddy, I left the bike and found a way through the reed-beds till the water was before me like a secret place. Gathered in the mouth of the smaller river, just resting on the water, were swans — nine-and-fifty of them, like Yeats's flock at Coole. Lots were youngsters with brownish plumage showing through the white, so I wondered if this was a gathering of those too young to breed, a club for adolescent swans. Now one would rear and beat its wings, then settle again on the choppy water.

I'd seen my ospreys, and the gathering of swans, and satisfied I turned to head for home again. Walking back to the bike I happened to glance upward, and there, flying toward me, was something huge, something I knew I had never seen before. The hair crept on the back of my neck and I fumbled to get the binoculars back out again. As it approached, it was like a brittle flying stick, side-on, growing thicker as it neared. It flew hugely and slowly, and looked as if it would pass directly overhead. I knelt down on the earth to make myself small, and steadied myself to focus the glasses on it, all the while telling myself to be calm, to look carefully and remember. It was big. Look at the wings, I told myself: straight and rectangular, with black and fingery ends. See how it's flying — not like a heron, not with heavy, confident wing-beats, but more . . . shivery. As it passed right over my head, it was the strangest thing, a weird cross-shape. I swivelled round on my knees to watch it travel southward over the fields and the village. It seemed to be making toward the pass in the hills the motorway takes, and the binoculars foreshortened the image, making the hills stand forward and loom bigger as the bird moved against them. Then it turned side-on, and its flight was almost tremulous for one so big. In profile, I could see clearly the head held far out on a neck so long and fragile it might snap, and the long legs and feet extended just as far behind.

Like some medieval peasant granted a vision, I was kneeling in a field, fixated by this uncanny cross in the sky. Then, as it moved slowly out of sight, I raced for home excited as a child, holding its image in my head like a bowlful of blue water — mustn't spill a drop.

This is what I want to learn: to notice, but not to analyse. To still the part of the brain that's yammering, "My god, what's that? A stork, a crane, an ibis? — don't be silly, its just a weird heron." Sometimes we have to hush the frantic inner voice that says "Don't be stupid," and learn again to look, to listen. You can do the organising and redrafting, the diagnosing and identifying later, but right now, just be open to it, see how it's tilting nervously into the wind, try to see the colour, the unchancy shape — hold it in your head, bring it home intact.

There is an RSPB reserve some twenty miles away, and I called the warden there. He was warm in his enthusiasm. Probably a common crane, though not so common here, only ten had ever been recorded in the county. They breed in Scandinavia, so it had wandered a long way on its long, nervy wings.

I watch the peregrines. On my desk the binoculars are closer to hand than the phone, than any reference book. If I swivel my chair and lift the binoculars, I can see them. It's becoming a tic. I remind myself of two friends, one who lays his mobile phone on the pub table, or surreptitiously in his pocket, and checks for messages. The other has trouble with her contact lenses and glances sideways for long moments as she's speaking, until the lenses float back over the iris and she can see clearly again. I don't know if either are aware they're doing it. How many times a day I glance through the glasses at the peregrine's ledge, I don't know. Could be thirty, could be a hundred.

I'm worried about them, though. When you'd think they should be sitting on eggs, both were often on view. Now, I haven't seen either for days.

J.A. Baker says, if you can't see the falcon, look up, and though I scan the sky I see nothing but grey clouds, and I wonder instead about J.A. Baker. Who was this man who could spend ten years following peregrines? Had he no job? Perhaps he was landed gentry. What allowed him to crawl the fields and ditches all day, all winter, until he could tell just by a tension in the air that there was a peregrine in the sky? His book is full, tremulous, overwrought, hungry. He writes like a falcon must see and so allows us to see, too. I walked up through sloping fields of coconut-scented whin, onto the crest of the hill, and watched a pair of buzzards wheel and cry above me, so close I could see her beak open as she mewed, and the pale, barred undersides of her wings.

This is the paradox: here is a person who would annihilate himself and renounce his fellows, who would enter into the world of birds and woods and sky, but then in an act of consummate communication to his human kind, step back into language and write a book still spoken of forty years on.

The RSPB man urged me to write to the county bird recorder with a description of my crane, and I did. The bird recorder — an amateur position — is an ornithologist who gathers and collates sightings and reports sent by other bird-watchers in the county. The recorder emailed back a friendly reply, saying my sighting would be circulated to the rarities committee and "judged." I imagine them at once, these judges of bird-sightings, bewigged and beaked like young owls. He attached last year's bird report for the county, "In case you're interested." I am, though pushed to explain why. It pleases me to know that on September 12, at Braco, were gathered 119 mistle thrushes, or that a crossbill was present in the Black Wood of Rannoch. It's what Louis MacNeice speaks of — the world being "incorrigibly plural."

Out of the window this dull morning, four or five crows were harassing not a peregrine, but an osprey, which was making, with steady beats, along the hillside. The osprey twitched at the crows, tilted, recovered and continued in its purposeful flight. The male peregrine turned up at exactly ten to three. I had to leave to fetch the kids from school, and glanced with the glasses just in time to see the resident jackdaws waft upward as he jinked through them and arrive at his stance. He stood for a few minutes, preened a little, then was gone again. It's the first time I'd seen either in days and I'm beginning to wonder if they're nesting at all.

~

April went out like a lion, with storm rains and winds. I'm sure now there's something wrong. The peregrine's ledge has an unlived-in, derelict air, a dock leaf twirls in the wind. "Keep watching!" the bird recorder had said, cheerfully, and I've been watching for four days now, but seen neither peregrine. It seems they have vanished into thin air. It happens — the Bird Report records only two pairs of peregrines attempting to nest in the entire county. Both failed. I may be wrong, I often am, but the peregrines' plinth is losing its specialness, just becoming part of the rockface again. If I was J.A. Baker, I'd feel the absence of their gaze.

Gales blew up during the evening. Dark fell early. From the front windows we watched black clouds driving down the estuary, but the back gardens were a tropical sight; trees and bushes in their full green bent and swayed. I slept badly, hearing the wind banging in the chimneys. In the morning the radio reported that gusts of 100mph had blown over Cairngorm, but at four I had been lying awake, wondering about birds. There are many things to fret about in the small hours, but never before have I worried about the tensile strength of an osprey's nest, atop its swaying pine.

By morning, the rain had blown over but still the wind blew. I was fetching the children's school clothes out of the tumble dryer, when I chanced to look out of the window and saw the male osprey himself, taking the same route eastward as he had before. He was again following the line of the hill, but then, with difficulty, he turned into the wind and began to tilt and battle against the gusts. His underwings looked very white when he banked, the tips dark and splayed. Two or three crows made half-hearted sorties toward the osprey, but they were minor nuisances and the big bird flicked them away. He looked as though he was trying to get enough lift to carry him up and over the summit. There's a fishing loch over there stocked with trout, a fast-food takeaway for a bird like this. Then the osprey was gone and I turned back to the dryer, looking for matching socks.

***

What pleases about the ospreys is the quiet success of their return to their rightful place. A damage remedied, a change of direction in our attitudes, as the bird itself makes the turn into the prevailing wind. These were native birds, but they were hunted to extinction in the nineteenth century. Then, in the mid-twentieth, they began to creep back, and with human help the osprey have now re-established 150 nest sites in Scotland, and even one in England. Some sites are famous; they are public spectacles with viewing places and video link-ups. There are large road signs directing us to birds' nests, and we don't find this bizarre. I like knowing these things. I like being able to glance up from my own everyday business, to see the osprey or the peregrine going about hers.

The crane was strange, out of place, a huge cross trembling in the air, the stuff of omens and portents. It made me excited and edgy for a couple of days. I await my "judgment." With the peregrines, though, it's something else: not the falconer's worship of mastery, not a wish to identify with terror, with the predator over its prey. What it is about the peregrines is their rarity. I'm sure they're gone now, but for a while I enjoyed the pleasure of a warm secret: I could watch this uncommon and handsome bird from my own window, and know it was there. J.A. Baker uses the word "flicker." The peregrine flickers at the edge of one's senses, at the edge of the sky, at the edge of existence itself.

Last night, when long shadows lay across the fields and the evening sky, winnowed by the wind, was whitish blue, I cycled out to check whether the ospreys' nest had indeed survived the gale, but a man was lying in the way. He was flat on his back on the path, ankles crossed, his hands neatly linked on his chest. A tobacco tin was sticking out of his trouser pocket, and he was drunk as a lord. Like one enchanted, he was gazing up through the branches of some pines. The rooks who live there were perplexed and they hung cawing in the wind as they looked down at the prostrate man who was looking up at them. I gave the man a wide berth, and cycled on.

Findings

Bone is subtle and lasting

GEORGE MACKAY BROWN

I hacked off the gannet's head with my penknife, which turned into one of those jobs you wish you'd never started. It was a Swiss army knife, with a blade only two inches long, and a diving gannet can enter the water at 90 mph: they have strong necks. It was early morning, low tide, and I was glad to have the beach to myself. When the head was at last free, I rolled the body with my foot. It was light and dense at once, still with much of its plumage, but the white breast was dirty and the black-tipped wings bedraggled. No doubt it was an Ailsa Craig gannet because it was washed ashore on Arran. Then I left the body among the dried wrack and shell-grit, and took the head home in my bag.

It was the skull I wanted, a sculptural form, the sightless sockets and that great piercing bill. I could picture it mounted in a glass box and hung on the wall or, better, displayed on the low table here in my study. Phil, my husband, had made the table from a huge piece of oak he hauled out of the Firth. Two hefty, deeply weathered supports were each joined with six through-tenons to the single board of the top. The top is a slab an inch and a quarter thick, but light-coloured. A bird's skull would sit well on such solid oak. Phil reckons it must have been a pier stanchion, before it came journeying downriver to wash up among the reeds. It was so big he couldn't lift it, he had to tie it fast, wait till the incoming tide, then float it on a rope behind him to the slipway. There he sawed it into three, before he could get it home piece by piece in a rucksack. "Like carrying a fridge," he said.

I put the gannet's head in a jar in the outhouse and poured over it a solution of caustic soda. When we were kids, we used to shine pennies with HP sauce or Coca-Cola. I had a notion that caustic soda would dissolve the skin and flesh, but leave the bones intact. Nothing happened. Daily, I stirred the mess with a stick, but the gannet merely bobbed up to glare at me from the pot, the feathers still adhering to the skin of its skull. Eventually the bones didn't clean but softened, and the liquid turned a foul brown-green and, gagging, I tipped the lot into a hole in the flowerbed.

But there was Phil's table and, on it, two white sticks I'd found at the east end of Loch Avich. There were thousands washed up there of these irresistible white sticks. They weren't straight like magic wands or conductors' batons, but sinuous like eels. I'd chosen two and left a whole strand of them behind. According to Norse mythology, the first woman and first man were fashioned from two sticks of ash washed up on a strand, and I remember thinking about that as I pleutered about on the loch's shore, holding this stick and then that up to the evening light, and deciding between them.

A gannet's skull would be good to have. Or a whaup's, but bird skulls are rare to find. I dare say most sea birds die at sea, and their weightless bones are pulverised by the water or the wind.

Once, on a flawless sandy beach in Donegal, I found five silver fishes, freshly abandoned by a wave, glittering and bright as knives presented in a canteen.

The yacht *Annag* was riding at anchor in the Sound of Shillay. The Sound separates two of the Monach Islands, Shillay itself and Ceann Iar, and although the sound was sheltered from the wind, the yacht was rolling and I was climbing over her side, clinging to what I'd learned to call the shrouds.

We hadn't intended to come here — in truth, I'd never heard of the Monach Islands before, but I lowered myself down the red plastic ladder toward the inflatable. We'd hoped to reach St Kilda but, as the skipper noted gruffly, nothing's guaranteed in this life. He was an awk-shaped man called Donald Wilkie. The wind persisted too much in the east for St Kilda, and he was going to anchor here for the day. Meanwhile, we could go ashore if we wanted to, and see what the morrow brought.

Suddenly, the yacht's side heaved upward and the tender dropped away, a yard of sea water opened beneath me and I took fright. Donald shouted above the wind, telling me to tuck round behind him, and make room for the others. When they were both aboard he started the engine, moved away from the yacht's white sides and turned toward shore. Sea water splashed over the prow and swilled around our feet, rain blew into our faces. We were all cowled in waterproofs and Donald looked especially monkish, as he stood at the tiller: a seafaring monk in a yellow habit.

From their haul-out on the rocks ahead, grey seals watched our approach. Sometimes on the yacht, during a brief lull in the wind, we had heard them singing their sad whoops, each to each, but now we could barely hear ourselves speak above the engine. The seals seemed not to mind our coming, but as we neared, a party of eider drakes put out into the waves. We rode so low on the water in the inflatable, it was the island that looked as though it were being pumped up, swelling and assuming what shape it had. It was a low, uninhabited place ringed with dunes and pale sands. When we reached the shore, Donald used the thrust of the engine to hold the boat against the rocks just long enough for us to clamber out, find our footing and struggle up onto the grass.

I'd never set foot in a yacht before this trip, never sailed the sea in anything smaller than a CalMac ferry, never approached land from the sea without a harbour and a town and all the panoply of human activity — stacked creels, diesel fumes, a church on a hill with a fish-shaped weather vane. I'd never understood you can draw a straight line across the ocean and call it a course. Ceann Iar is uninhabited by people but birds were breeding here, the air was worked by oystercatchers, fulmars, terns, and there were many rabbits, and sheep.

When we were all three ashore, Donald turned the tender and headed back over the waves to his yacht. I stood for a few minutes, following his progress, letting the movement of the sea settle in my ears. Martin and Tim were taking off their red life jackets and zipping them round the horizontal bars of a sheep fank, so they couldn't blow away. Maybe this is where the sheep are shorn. There were dollops of fleece at our feet, too rain-sodden to be blown away, though the wind blew strong.

The water we'd crossed was ink-blue, flecked with white, but calmer there in the sound than out in open water. Beyond the sound, waves barged westward. It was raining steadily. In this place of water and horizons and flat green islands, there was only one vertical line: Shillay lighthouse. Rain beat at my left side, and wind buffeted me, as I raised the binoculars and looked across the channel. Something had disturbed a colony of Arctic terns at the foot of the lighthouse. The birds moved in the wind in and out and around each other, but the gantry round the light, 100 feet higher — that was a ravens' place. A pair were hanging blackly in the wind, against the grey sky. When I lowered the glasses, the yacht seemed terribly small between the two islands, with its white mast and shrouds, small, and fragile as the skull of a bird.

My two companions on this sortie hadn't met before this trip, but happened both to be sound recordists; one, Tim Dee, is a producer for BBC Radio; Martin Leitner works for the Austrian state broadcasting company. In waterproof bags they'd brought microphones, tape recorders and binoculars. Both were keen on birds. In the five or six days we spent together, I grew to appreciate the company of people who listen to the world. They don't feel the need to talk all the while. They were alert to bird-cries, waves sucking on rocks, a rope frittering against a mast. Sometimes I'd notice them catch each other's eye, give a complicit smile, and I'd wonder what I'd missed.

Beside the sheep fanks was the shepherds' bothy, no bigger than an allotment shed, and beside it lay three huge round floats like Space Hoppers. The rain was turning heavy now, but we began walking over the machair, inland into the wind. Few flowers bloomed under our feet, just tiny yellow sea pansies. We'd no plan but to spend a few hours exploring until, at a prearranged time, we'd return to the landing place to be collected. But the air was full of birds. Tim knew most about them. "What are those?" I could ask of a flight of shore birds. "Dunlin, a few turnstones," he'd call back. Once I looked back to see him on bended knee, in his blue cagoule, looking through binoculars at the waves. "Great northern divers — in summer plumage!" He could tell a bird by a mark, a piped note, an attitude in the air. When I marvelled at this, he said identifying a bird was similar to making a poem or a finished piece of work from the kind of notes I stopped to make in my book, crouched down out of the wind. It was he who saw, in a grassy rut, the handful of fluff that was a lapwing chick while its parents flipped in the air overhead; he who pointed out the way the starlings launched themselves mob-handed into the wind.

We walked between dunes that were bound by bent grass. The island is so low that from the top of the dunes we could survey it all, a couple of miles of machair, marshy sumps, sandy hillocks. Once, Martin grabbed me midstep, and once I did the same for him, because what had seemed mere pebbles had snapped into focus as three olive-green eggs cupped in eiderdown. The eggs were covered in greenish shit, to deter marauders. More than once, we crunched on rabbit bones among the sharp grass. There was a lamb, very new, with its stomach opened by buzzards. But as one or the other of us stopped to check something in our binoculars, or turn over some bit of flotsam with a foot, we each took to walking alone, each into the wind.

On Donald's sea charts, Ceann Iar appears less like a rounded treasure island than a flayed skin. It's a place of wide bays and dunes, a low interruption of the sea. Ceann Iar means "West Head," and it's joined at low tide to the isle called Stockay, and thence to its eastern twin, Ceann Ear. These plus Shillay and some smaller rocks make up the group called the Monachs. There used to be plenty of people here, crofters and cottears who kept black cows, and the islands were famed for their fertility, but now there is no one left. I worked my way down to a southern-facing bay, and trudged along the tideline, where there would be no danger of standing on nests. Midway down the pale sand, where the retreating tide had left it, lay a band of orange weed: thick ribbons, like tagliatelle. Sometimes as I walked, I'd flush a flock of feeding shore birds, dunlin or turnstones. I loved the moment when, after they'd all risen together, they all banked at once, like when you pull the string in a Venetian blind.

What do we imagine, those of us who don't live there, of uninhabited Hebridean islands? Windswept, we might say; remote, all vast skies and seascapes, machair and tiny yellow flowers. From where I stood on the beach, a long finger of rock ran out into the sea, waves broke against it and there were seals hauled out there, too. The rain, of course, didn't bother them. You could tell seal from rock only by the sheen and shape of their bodies. These were grey seals, with Roman noses. They slump on the rocks, and don't bend themselves up at each end as common seals do. "Like black bananas," the B&B lady had said on Berneray, the night before we sailed. We'd been watching common seals through her double-glazed picture window, a window that slammed out the wind and reduced the outside world to a spectacle: soundless, windless, with no smell or tang. The B&B couple had retired to Berneray from Essex. "We love it here," they said. God knows, if I lived here, I thought, as I battled along the shore, I'd have double glazing too.

A stone caught my eye and I bent to pick it up. It was a perfect sphere of white quartz that fitted the palm of my hand. "Orb" was the word that came to mind. I'll keep that, I thought and in the moment it had taken me to admire it and slip it into my bag all the seals had slithered from their rocks into the water. Two-dozen heads, two-dozen pairs of dark eyes were looking at me, the human figure on the wide shore. Then, on a whim, they all dived, leaving only splashes, as though a handful of pebbles had been thrown into a pond.

Walking in this way in the rain, head down into the rain and wind, I didn't see the whale until I was next to it. It didn't startle me — it was too big and too dead to be startling. My body was still carrying the rocking motion of the yacht, which feels a bit like shock, or like being drunk but still able to think. My mind continued its rocking and announced, Oh, it's a whale. A small whale. I was standing by the head. The head came up to my knees. I looked up onto the dunes, scanned the length of the long curved beach and, had one of the others been in sight I'd have called, but no one was there.

It must have been on the shore a month or two, the whale, because it was half-blanketed in the orange-coloured weed. Half sinking or half emerging out of a bed of sand and weed. The body was rolled in the motion of a wave, and there was one dark orifice, like a cave, in its mouldering head, perhaps an eye socket. It was the heaviest creature I had ever seen, dead and out of the water's buoyancy, a massive failure. I thought about touching it, with just one finger, furtively, the way a gull pecks, and I wish now I had, because I've never touched a whale and probably won't get the chance again. I should have touched the skin, because it looked almost like black leatherette. The biggest leatherette sofa you can imagine, washed up on an empty shore. There was no smell, or if there was it was lost to the wind and rain. But the sand around the whale was marked with soft triangles — the webbed feet of herring gulls. It wasn't bloody, where they had managed to peck through the skin, but the tissue had the foamy texture of worm-rotten wood. Partly because I didn't know quite what to do with myself — some gesture seemed required and I didn't know what — I slowly paced it out. Twenty-five feet or so, a minke perhaps. As the rain fell on myself and the whale, and the surf roared, I stood wondering whether it had stranded and died here, or been washed up dead in a storm.

A shout, a wave, a lean figure in blue and green waterproofs. Martin was hailing me from a sand dune, a few hundred yards away. "Look," he said. "I've found a plane — a bit of a plane." His accent was Austrian, but his English near-perfect, witty, idiomatic. "Come and see."

Together we slithered down into a cleft between dunes, and then he was bending over a shapely piece of metal, his long back damp with rain. I couldn't see his face for the side of his hood, but he was calling back to me, "See — the ailerons still work!" The wind knocked me, so I couldn't quite make out what he was doing, but he seemed to be pulling at a wire sticking out of the sand, and a little metal flap waggled up and down obligingly. Then he stood and swept his arm.

"Can you believe all this plastic — all these floats, bottles? All this plastic rope!"

The cleavages between the sand dunes, where the wind and waves had driven it, were choked with plastic. If it got beyond the rampart of dunes, it was strewn across the flat of the island. There were hundreds of marker-buoys, ripped from their creels. The same storms that lobbed rocks 200 yards inland had strewn floats and bottles and plastic crates. Among the dunes and bent grass, at the mouths of rabbit holes, trapped in every cove, were tangles of rope and plastic bottles, shoes and aerosol cans. Martin was lifting something battered and red from a heap of weed. "What's this, in English?" he called.

"Bollard," I said. "Traffic cone. Is there any more of this plane?"

"I haven't found any. But I want to see your whale!"

They had their own fascination, the shampoo and milk cartons, the toilet-cleaner bottles we could turn over with our feet. Though the colours were faded and the labels long gone, we knew their shapes, had seen them ranked in supermarkets and hardware stores. Brushes, masking tape, training shoes, orange polypropylene net: weeks later, in a sunlit street café in Edinburgh, Donald explained the currents to me, moving his huge hands over the table as if his coffee cup were the island. This shore caught it. At the tideline of every inlet, where the dunlin foraged and fulmars rested, were seals' vertebrae and whalebones, driftwood and plastic garbage. I wonder now if we shouldn't have been more concerned about the plane. A plane had crashed, sometime, and we were unconcerned. Little wonder, when there were winds and currents strong enough to flense whales and scatter their bones across the machair. Here in the rain, with the rotting whale and wheeling birds, the plastic floats and turquoise rope, the sealskins, driftwood and rabbit skulls, a crashed plane didn't seem untoward. If a whale, why not an aeroplane? If a lamb, why not a training shoe? Here was a baby's yellow bathtime duck, and here the severed head of a doll. The doll still had tufts of hair, and if you tilted her she blinked her eyes in surprise.

We were soaked, the wind was climbing and we'd had enough of Ceann Iar. It was a deathly place, this island, and it was nearly time for Donald to return in the tender and take us back to the yacht.

We found the door to the plane on the northern side of the island. Just the door, insulated with four inches of yellowish foam. Blubber, if you like. Near the door, Martin found a whale's scapula, a flat rounded triangle of bone, and when he held it triumphantly on his head he looked like one of those Tibetan monks with the yellow crest on their hats. I slithered down a dune to retrieve a whale's vertebra from a tussock. The hole where the nerves pass sheltered some yellow sea pansies.

This is what we chose to take away from Ceann Iar: a bleached whale's scapula, not the door of a plane; an orb of quartz, not a doll's head. As for Tim, he'd picked up a two-foot-long plastic duck, which he carried under his arm. So we walked the mile back to the sheep pens, the rain at our backs. The thin pencil of the lighthouse was our way-sign. A long time ago, there used to be a monastery on these islands, where the lighthouse stands; a convent, too. To the seals who watched from the water, we must have looked less like monks than cheapskate Magi, the three of us in waterproofs, one behind the other, bearing these peculiar things.

Below decks on the yacht, it was wood-lined and dark and crowded, like a Victorian parlour. There was a foldaway dining table and above it, a brass lamp tied with elastic that nonetheless swung as the boat rocked. The barometer slid against the wall. We spent the rest of the afternoon sitting on narrow benches around the table, or up under the spray-hood, reading or watching the sea. On a little pocket above the chart-desk, next to the pilot and first-aid manuals, was a back number of the *Hebridean Naturalist*. In it I read that one beach in New Zealand already has plastic sand — 100,000 grains to every square metre. The author of the article had found, on a beach in Lewis, an otter garrotted by plastic tape. He reckoned the strangest thing he'd ever discovered on a shore was the severed head of a donkey.

In Alasdair Alpin MacGregor's delightful account of these islands, he says that the people used bent grass from the dunes, the very grass that trapped the plastic bottles and polyprop net, to make mats, rope, horse collars, heavy baskets and sacks: "So thickly plaited were the sacks of Heiskeir bent that the weavers of them boasted of their having been virtually impervious to rain or sea-spray." "Sea-spoil" he calls the flotsam, but he meant the driftwood that the crofters valued and were quick to collect.

We read or sketched or fiddled with tapes and equipment. Donald showed me how the boat's equipment worked, the autopilot and GPS systems. Two small computer screens were angled above the chart-desk, but the charts themselves, the ones he favoured, were Victorian. He'd had to go especially to the National Library in Edinburgh to get a copy of these old charts. To make them, he said, two men had had to put out in a rowing boat and row — "row, mind you" — up and down in straight lines over the open sea. Every cable, that is, every tenth of a mile, they lowered a lead on a line, and discovered both the depth in fathoms and what composed the sea bed, be it sand or gravel or rock. All these were noted on the chart, in a meticulous and precise script. The sea was a tight grid of readings, the land bare. With a magnifying glass we found the tiny anchor that marked the spot where we lay.

As the afternoon passed, the wind mounted up through the scale. Every so often the radio fizzed and the Stornoway coast-guard, in beautiful and courteous tones, alerted, "All stations, all stations," and issued another gale warning. Force 7 through 8, "Soon," she said, or "Imminent." By about five o'clock, it was up to severe gale force 9, veering southeast. We groaned or laughed. Donald clamped his hand to his bald head. Soon, im-minently, the wind, already moaning through the rigging, raised its pitch. The sound-men smiled, and began reaching for their tape recorders. Suddenly an alarm bleeped above the chart-desk. "We're dragging anchor," said Donald. "I know a better an-chorage for such a wind, on the other side of the island. After we've eaten, we'll move."

We manoeuvred the yacht carefully into a bay where a pale beach was backed by dunes. The echo sounder showed only seven foot of depth; leaning over the guard rail, we could see the sand ghostly-green through the water. "How much depth?" Donald shouted from the wheel. He seemed to prefer our human judgment to the echo sounder. "How much now?" We moved carefully in toward shore, the comfort of land.

It had been inhabited once. A single abandoned house stood at the westernmost end of the bay. It had no roof and its twin gables rose against the grey sky as if surrendering. It drew the eye, as the lighthouse had. Maybe there's something instinctive in us, that we're drawn to human habitation and can't resist a ruin, the way newborn babies respond to a crude drawing of a face. These are the rarities in human history, the places from which we've retreated. These once-inhabited places play a dif-ferent air to the uninhabited; they suggest the lost past, the lost Eden, not the Utopia to come. Under the spray-hood, we were out of the wind and could sit as the boat turned, listening to the wind. We were only 200 yards offshore. "You see? Only 200 yards out and it's rolling like this. Imagine what it's like on the open water," Donald insisted, as though we didn't believe him.

"But it's a lee shore, you realise that? Not ideal, but the wind's forecast to veer to south, then it'll be okay." Till then, though, if the anchor dragged or the chain snapped we'd be driven on-shore. Land doesn't mean safety to a mariner. Land means danger. What you want is to be swept out to sea."

All night the wind shrieked in the rigging, but it was easy to sleep, cradled in the rocking boat. In the morning, with the boat still riding tense in the wind, Donald announced that we wouldn't be moving. The lamp swung, the barometer slid back and forth against the wall. It was better to be out in the cockpit, watching the wind-flecked grey sea and the birds. A shag issued up from the water. Gannets, that class act, banked now low across the surface, now gaining height to dive, closing their immense black-tipped wings against the grey sky. In certain lights, only the wing tips would show; in others, the gleam of the diving back and a spout of water. Two or three times we witnessed skua attacks, a dark shape that twisted down among terns then lifted away over the dunes. By mid-morning, the sky had begun to clear, the colours to reveal themselves: blue for the sky and water. The islands were green dunes, ringed with palest cream sand. Still, however, gale warning followed gale warning, and then the radio brought a new woman's voice, this time from the Benbecula missile base. In mellifluous tones she warned shipping of missile-testing, at a certain hour.

"We're out of range," said Donald, but nonetheless poked a button on the radio, told the missile base that we were anchored here. The woman's voice, borne on fizz, assured us with courtesy that we were indeed out of range and, besides, the wind was such they'd thought the better of missile-testing themselves.

"Missiles? That must have been what I found." said Martin.

"Where?" Donald barked.

"On the island, a big metal tube, about this long . . ."

The last crofters had left the largest island, Ceann Ear, in the 1940s. Some houses still stand on the eastern side of the island, looking over the sea to the low hills of North Uist. There is a school, and the walls of some old tumbledown black houses, where nettles and silverweed grow. Fulmars nest in their corners now, and there are nests of cheeping starlings in the crannies of the stonework. We had come ashore again, this time to Ceann Ear, but though the wind was still restless and strong it had stopped raining and the world again seemed habitable. There was the constant muffled roar of surf. This island seemed a place of life compared to yesterday's, but still we offered the prize of a Mars bar to the finder of the first carcass. At the top of the beach, on the crest of the ramp of sea-worn stones, lay a stranded lobster creel, and beside it a mottled grey seal pup, who tilted back its head and crooned. A pace away an eider duck sat tight on her nest between a few stones. She faced into the wind, her back rose softly as she breathed, her plumage was rippled with the same grey as the rocks around her, the lichen and fawn-coloured grass.

Again we spread out, and were soon lost to each other. This island was marshy in the middle, and oyster-catchers went piping overhead, and near the abandoned houses was a freshwater loch with a pair of swans. I'd read that the only freshwater creatures on this island, apart perhaps for some sticklebacks, were eels all the way from the Sargasso. I looked in the narrow burns as I jumped them, but saw none. The Mars bar went to Tim, whom I found trying to break the leg off a rotting herring gull, which had crash-landed into a dune. The gull had been ringed, and he wanted the ring to send back to the British Museum in London. I offered him my Swiss army knife, saying, "You can take the head off a gannet with this." Later, he appeared in the distance below a weaving colony of terns, holding up a microphone like a Statue of Liberty at the edge of a new land.

I was lying on my back on the landward side of a high embankment of pebbles looking up at the same terns which squealed and weaved around each other as they looked down at me. Such fine, elfin creatures. There must have been nests among the stones, but for the life of me I couldn't see any. Above the wheeling birds the grey sky was breaking to blue. Out of the wind, under the sun, it was almost warm. Before me, in a dip in the land, was a very small loch where flag irises would soon be in bloom. A white plastic tub was trapped among their stems.

The islands are a twenty-first-century midden of aerosols and plastic bottles, and I was thinking about what we'd valued enough to keep. It seemed that what we chose to take — the orb of quartz, the whalebones — were not the things that endured, but those that had been transformed by death or weather. Sure, we retain the useful — Donald saw lasting value in his Victorian charts. "No one now would put such work into the task," he said. George MacKay Brown once wrote that "the past was a like a great ship that has gone ashore, and archivist and writer must gather as much of the rich squandered cargo as they can." But we pick and choose, and I wondered if it's still possible to value that which endures, if durability is still a virtue, when we have invented plastic, and the doll's head with her tufts of hair and rolling eyes may well persist after our own have cleaned back down to bone.

I was lying on the stones, thinking these idle thoughts, when a quad bike appeared and growled across the machair a couple of hundred yards in front of me, rose up over a dune and disappeared.

The shepherd's face was thin, unshaven and deeply lined — vertical lines, like weathered oak. He was dressed in blue overalls. His eyes under his black beret were also blue. We met on the strandline of a beach. He told me he had been on the island for seventeen days, alone, and would soon leave. He was fetching driftwood for his fire and had loaded onto a trailer towed by his quad bike a wormy log; rather, a third of a wormy log, because he'd had to saw it into pieces to get it back. I presume he was staying in the old schoolhouse, because that was the only one of the island's buildings still with a roof, and in a pit outside old tin cans were half-buried. I asked the shepherd about the marvellous number of creel-markers and buoys strewn across the islands, and he answered with the meticulous English of the Gael:

"They are without value. I have told the fishermen there are plenty here, but they say they are without value. If they were of any value," he laughed, "they would be gone."

It was Martin who gave me the gannet's skull. I have it here, in my study at the top of the house, on the table my husband made from the pier-stanchion he'd had to cut into three and brought home without the aid of a quad bike.

We had sailed from the low, bone-strewn, gale-swept dunes of Monach Islands, to the isle of Scarp, and were sitting on the yacht's cockpit in a silent, calm evening, anchored between high islands of cliff and stone. It was about ten at night, still daylight, and a huge three-quarter moon had risen above the island. The moon was so bright we could see with binoculars its every crater. A single wren was singing from the cliffs. Primroses clung to the damp earth beside a waterfall that splashed down into the sea. In this anchorage the water was so still, so emerald green that when an arctic tern flew over, its plumage absorbed the green of the water and it became a green bird. The first time I saw this, I nearly called Tim to come outside because I thought I was looking at some exotic from the Amazon. There was nothing on the little beach here but yellow sand, a few shells and otter tracks.

Martin had found the bones on Ceann Iar, but chose this moment to produce them, with mock ceremony, from the inner pocket of his jacket. Mock ceremony because — the others were laughing — we had just been watching the arctic tern bring gifts of food to his intended, who sat disdainfully on a rock. With the air of a magician Martin produced first one leg bone, then another, then a tiny white complex affair which, held in a certain way, was exactly the shape of the purple orchid flowers we'd found on the hill that afternoon. Lastly, he handed me the skull. In truth, it was not a whole skull, but the lower mandible, bleached clean. I was laughing too, but managed to thank him gravely, and at once, before they got broken, I made an ossuary of the plastic Tupperware box where I kept my tobacco.

"How did you know I wanted one?" I asked.

"You told me," he said. "On Ceann Iar."

⁓

On the table made of the washed-up pier-stanchion are two pale sticks, like eels, or the first man and the first woman. There's the gannet's shank, its tiny orchid-shaped bone, and the whale's vertebra. These are in my study. Tim had celebrated his birthday on the yacht, and as a present I'd given him the orb of quartz. The bits of aeroplane, traffic cone and whale will still be on the shores of the Monach Islands. The penknife, the one I'd used to cut off the original gannet's head, is presently in my handbag. I'd found it — did I mention this? — one spring day on a beach in Fife. The gannet's beak is beside me here. Holding it up to the window light, I've just noticed a tiny bit of feather still clinging to the bone. I wish now I'd brought home the doll's head too. I'd have put her on a corner of my desk like a paperweight, with her mad tufts of hair and those sea-blue blinking eyes.

The Braan Salmon

What you notice, when you enter the little chamber, is the roaring of the waterfalls. It's much louder inside than out. The chamber, they call it Ossian's Hall, is built on a rocky bluff which reaches out over the falls. A damp elegant room, it opens onto a half-moon balcony, and you can stand on the balcony admiring the scene as the spray and updraught dampens your face. Apparently, in its heyday, a couple of hundred years ago, the walls were lined with mirrors to reflect the falls, so the Duke of Atholl and his guests could enjoy the sublime river sound and the peat-tinged, spumy water cascading all about them. A little Romantic eco-art installation.

The Braan, a Highland river, is short, fast and rocky. Tall Douglas firs and beeches grow from its banks. Directly below the balcony, the river folds itself down between buttresses of rock. The drop is not great, no more than twenty feet in total — it's hard to judge from above. But today the water was hammering down at a tremendous force. The salmon have to jump against this weight of water. You don't have to wait long, leaning out over the balcony rails, before you see a salmon hurl itself out of the foam, into the useless air, only to drop back. The length of a man's arm, or a woman's arm, they try again, two, three, four at a time, only to be dashed back. For a long moment they hang in the air, like dancers. It was said of Nijinsky that, when he leapt, he seemed to stop in midair, and the fish do that: leap, hold themselves in the air, pink bellies and speckled green backs, then fall back to vanish with a twist into the foam as the river crashes over the falls, and the spray dampens your face. From this balcony, this viewpoint, we can be as concerned or as indifferent as gods. Mostly we're concerned.

A photographer arrived with a tripod. We had to bend in toward each other to make out the other's words, but he told me he was teaching a week-long photography course and, sure enough, from among the trees on the river bank a half-dozen photographers with woolly hats and tripods quietly appeared. Below us, the salmon continued to jump and fall. As the photographer twisted the legs of his tripod into place, he said, "Amazing, isn't it? I wonder how often they can try before they're exhausted. Suppose it's the real survival of the fittest. If they don't make it then . . . Ho! Did you see that one?"

<hr />

"Ho!" is what we say when one of the salmon leaps. Ho! — a coinage somewhere between noble and heroic. I asked the photographer if he specialised in wildlife, and he said something I couldn't make out. Was it "wildscapes"? Did he tell me that in the winter he went to Finland to do bears?

Birch leaves were twirling down into the water. The rocks in the middle of the river were patted with their gentle shapes. The leaves twirled down, landed on the water, then were swept merrily, merrily over the falls and away. There was a lull, then Ho! — a leaping fish.

Once down the falls the water packs into a narrow linn and travels at speed until it's released into a wide pool. Spume swirls over the surface. There must be fish in there, backed up, feeling the water, waiting to move up to the front. On my way here, I'd passed a hapless lad with a fishing rod who was being questioned by two gruff men in green Barbour jackets. One had a notebook. The lad stood uncertainly between the bailiffs.

I read somewhere that before the invention of the bicycle, the salmon was the most efficient machine on the planet, power to weight. My bike was leaning against a tree, outside the little chamber. The photographer asked, "This you going your regular round? Bit of gut-thrashing on the bike, then replenish the soul here?"

"Something like that."

Away from the river, a pleasing silence fell. Siskins were working the trees. I cycled upriver a short way, below trees and out over some rough grazing, to the next bridge, Rumbling Bridge, where I leaned the bike on the parapet and looked down at the river. Something about the salmon was bothering me. Wherever I went today, be it cycling or fetching the kids from school, watching telly, or going to bed, they'd still be there, hurling themselves out of the water into the spray-filled air, empty air. What, I was wondering, were we admiring with all our Ho!-ing? Their apparent heroism, their endeavour? What we're pleased to call the human spirit. It seemed nature was prepared to wager the whole salmon project on a few individuals who can Ho! and keep on Ho!-ing until somehow they got up over the falls and back to their spawning grounds.

I crossed the upper bridge, then returned downstream by the south bank and back to to Ossian's Hall — no great distance. Replenish the soul. I stood again on the damp balcony, the river dinging in my ears. The photographer and his students were gone, but other people arrived. First came a very red-faced man with a blue tie. He looked out over the river below and seemed not to notice the fish leaping. Others, though, had come specially. Two softly spoken ladies in walking shoes and stout skirts arrived, and one asked me: "Have you been here long? Have you seen any? We'd heard they were here. Oh! Look at that! Did you see that one? What a shame . . ."

It was something the photographer had said that bothered me. A week-long photography course. And his students skulking among the trees, slightly farcical with their woolly hats and tripods. I had nearly asked him what a week-long photography course consisted of, but the river was too loud and I'd a hunch I knew already — it would be similar to the creative writing courses I teach myself. His would be all lenses and composition and f-stops and light meters. Wildscapes. How to make a better photograph of the natural world. How to master all that technical stuff but make the image look fresh, natural, accidental even. How to employ all that technique expressly to make the result look natural, techniqueless.

I leaned over the railings with the two ladies in tweeds, and began watching differently the expressionless fish. I was watching for technique. Of the first six to leap and hang suspended in the air, five seemed to be directing themselves at a particularily thick coil of water. Further, they seemed to be trying to get into the back of it, or maybe they were thrust there by the sheer force. When the softly spoken ladies moved away, a party of elderly men arrived, as they told me, from Kirkcaldy. A party of retired chums who went out for a walk together every Friday. They had walking sticks and backpacks; children and grandchildren, no doubt. We leaned out over the balcony rail together. "Ho!" and "Ho!" we said as the salmon leapt.

One man said, "They must start deep under."

"To get enough lift?"

"Aye —"

"Or down in the back water, get a run at it . . ."

"They seem to be going for that bit of water, the thickest bit."

"Less air. Maybe they need to get a bit of water, give the tail a wee flick, then . . ."

There was nothing for a moment but the onrush, then four salmon, one after the other, all cast themselves up, all intended for the left-hand edge, next to the rock. Again they were repulsed, one dashed off the rock, the others running out of speed and momentum. They hung for a moment in the air, speckled, pink-bellied, then fell away down.

Technique, or pure "Ho!"? How long did they spend sitting in the back-water, feeling the way ahead, feeling the speed and weight of water. Were any of these failed Ho-ing jumps reconnaissance trips? "Instinct," we're told. Most efficient power-to-weight organisms on the planet. Then a big one leapt clear out of the water, aiming at the left-hand edge, and it gained enough height to re-enter just where the water poured itself over a lip of rock. We couldn't see, couldn't quite make it out, but it looked like a success. An extra wee flick of the tail, enough momentum to defy gravity and the force of the water, a hidden ledge to rest on for a moment . . .

"Ho! There! One made it!" said the old men. "Did you see it? I'm pretty sure it did . . ."

Technique or "Ho!"? I dare say it was both. The technique hidden below the water, but in front of our eyes it looked like a piece of pure "Ho!"

In his hallway, our neighbour Robin Guthrie has a stuffed salmon in a glass case. He caught it himself, all 31 lb of it, last year on the River Earn. It was difficult enough hauling a two-stone fish up the muddy river bank, but "getting it across the field was the interesting bit." He first showed us the fish in the chest freezer in his cellar, and gave my husband and me some of the meat, which he'd had smoked, at Christmas time. The meat was the dark, opaque colour of topaz or cairngorm. Now the fish hangs motionless in its glass box, above a few black-painted polystyrene rocks. Its mouth is open, showing sharp narrow teeth. They had to remove the coat rack to accommodate the trophy. Sometimes, when Robin comes to babysit for us he brings his fly box, and spends the evening with a beer and the telly, tying bibios, silver Wilkinsons and blue charms: little artefacts intended to mimic a drowning moth, or larvae ascending through still water just after they hatch.

Our houses overlook the Firth of Tay. All the salmon of the upper rivers of the Tay and Earn, the Tilt and Garry and Braan, must have passed here, slipped past our windows, so to speak. Until quite recently salmon-fishing was a local industry. They used heavy rowing boats called cobles to pull nets across the river. Now the boats come out only for an annual race at the time of the Highland Games, in mid-June.

One evening late last summer, I was looking out of Robin's

kitchen window at the Firth, through some binoculars he'd found. He was going to hand them in as lost property, but first he was enjoying them. They were brilliant binoculars. Hundreds of pounds' worth of optics. I weighted them in my hand then lifted them to my eyes, and looked through the window to the river. Looked through the binoculars, then lowered them and looked with my own eyes. I lifted them, and lowered them, looked now with the glasses, now without.

"Have you seen the martins?" I asked.

Robin took the glasses, and it was true — with the binoculars we could see thousands of martins swooping over the water in the evening light, thousands of birds. Without the glasses, the sky was apparently empty.

"God, they're good."

"Makes you wonder what else is going on, doesn't it?"

I began telling Robin about the salmon on the Braan, how I'd been watching them attempting the falls, from the Ossian's Hall at the Hermitage.

"It's a wonder any of them manage it at all," I said. "They're so . . . heroic. Do any of them just fail? What happens if the water's really fast and none of them makes it?"

"On the Braan?" Robin said, laconically. "None of 'em."

"What?"

"None of them clear the falls. It's deliberate. It's not a natural salmon river. There are hatcheries upstream. That's why they put them on the Braan, just so the hatchlings couldn't return there and spawn."

I was gawping at him. "You mean it's some sort of joke?"

"Even if they got past the Hermitage, there is no way others could get up the falls at Rumbling Bridge. You've been there. It's just free-fall, a chasm. Nothing could get up that."

I put the binoculars back on the kitchen table.

"So what are they supposed to do? Die trying?"

"Nah, they give up eventually. Spawn downstream."

Not the survival of the fittest, as the photographer had thought, but the survival of the ones who give it up as a bad job and settle someplace quiet. A small life in the suburbs. Salmon wisdom.

"I don't get it," I said. "Why can't they come back? It's their instinct, isn't it?"

"They don't want the fish born there artificially returning to spawn, because it would mess up their studies. They're studying the hatchlings, how they get on, how they disperse and survive. If they came back as adults and spawned, they wouldn't know which was which. Which had been born in the tanks and which naturally."

"Oh," I said. "Do you think there are binoculars so good we could even see the flies the martins are chasing?"

———

They say the day is coming—it may already be here—when there will be no wild creatures. That is, when no species on the planet will be able to further itself without reference or negotiation with us. When our intervention or restraint will be a factor in their continued existence. Every creature: salmon, sand martins, seals, flies. What does this matter?

I'd written about watching the salmon leap before Robin's revelation, but after that I put the work aside, because something had changed in my attitude to the fish. Now I knew a secret, something the salmon didn't know, that whether it be instinct or technique it didn't matter, their effort was all hopeless. I thought about the little passing audience, the sheer goodwill of the viewers from the balcony; the photographer with his "wildscapes" and the old men from Kirkcaldy, and the mild ladies who said, "Are they here? We'd heard they were here. We came specially." Replenishing our souls. Joke. Ho Ho.

Could I "replenish my soul" by watching the salmon try to leap the falls, knowing all the while that it was useless? What could we do, that passing ad hoc community of salmon-watchers, burdened with this new knowledge, but shake our heads at their dumb efforts, and walk away? Or go walk up the Tilt, say, and watch the salmon leaping there, a fish identical in every way, which had survived the predations of seals and fisher-men, and found its way home, but was oddly superior, because "natural."

〜

Salmon find their way back to the river of their birth, we're told, by smell. This sounds both plausible and ludicrous. Plausible, in that how else could they do it? And ludicrous, like the idea that geese were born of barnacles, or that herons wax and wane with the moon. Salmon, feeding off the south coast of Greenland, in cold unimaginable depths one day give a wee flick of the tail and turn toward the smell of home. What, do we imagine, is the smell of the Braan? The smell that must distil on our faces, out of the spray, as we stand in that little balcony? Rather, how does the smell of the Braan differ from the smell of the Earn, say, or the Tilt? The water of the falls of the Braan must surely smell of schist and granite gravel, peat, and fish, alder, microbes and leaf rot, earth, silage, moss and oxygen? And a salmon can follow this smell like a dog who knows its way home from the pub.

〜

The winter passed into a long damp spring. Under the stuffed salmon in its glass case in Robin's hallway appeared a pram. We celebrated the birth of a daughter to him and his wife, Caroline; and, with high delight, another birth: to friends who'd endured failed gruelling cycles of IVF treatment until — Ho! — one tiny embryo took and stayed put.

Winter passed and I didn't think about the salmon again until today. It was already mid-April, but the first day warm enough to carry on its breeze the promise of summer. At lunch-time I cycled a mile downriver, across fields to the edge of the Firth, where stands a ruined fishing lodge. The lodge faces the estuary, and when I arrived the tide was at its lowest, exposing sandbanks all the way downriver towards the sea. There were horizontal bands of colour — mud flats, a thin channel of water, reed-beds on the far shore, a line of trees. Out on the first sandbank, six seals were hauled up to bask in sybaritic abandon. One was rolled on its back, warming its speckled belly in the sun. They were policed by two crows. Then, behind them, in a long thin line on a farther sandbank, were thousands of pink-footed geese, all taking a siesta. I could pan with the binoculars a distance of half a mile of exposed sand, and geese dozing along its length.

A light aircraft droned overhead, a lark rose in the ploughed field behind. In the half-hour I'd been there, the tide had turned and, noticeably, water was flooding in, a silent, almost menacing arrival. It would rise and touch the bodies of the sleeping seals, the pink feet of the geese. It was the seals that made me think of the salmon. I wondered if salmon were even now migrating upriver, slipping unseen past the seals on the flood tide. Was it the promise of salmon that had drawn the seals so far from the sea? They were beyond the point where the estuary water was still salt. A mile downriver, the bladderwrack stopped growing. None of our garden trees has this bright-orange lichen, splashed on the elders, this staneraw, which lives by salt.

Fish, following a smell, slipping past the sleeping seals, up past our town, past the house where I'd watched the martins last September, invisibly passing the windows where, even now, the two new mothers might be standing with their newborns in their arms. There were no martins; they were yet to arrive. A heron cronked overhead. Maybe those salmon making for the Braan could even smell in the river here a hint of plastic — the tanks they had been born into, two or three years before. Ach! Good for them, I thought, as I stood to go.

Water was slipping in, muddy tonnages of water. The seals ignored it but the geese were becoming restless, and in parties of six or ten they began to take off, strung out like lines of washing, till they cleared the reed-beds and gained enough height to turn off into the fields. I could hear them making their housewifely *wa-wa-wa*. Soon they'd be away, too, to their own breeding grounds far in the north.

Crex-Crex

On the wall of my room in the B&B is a print of Constable's *Haywain.* The room's pleasant, with floral curtains and bed-spread, a vase of silk flowers and a few prints on the walls. *The Haywain*'s only small, hardly the six-foot original, but you'd know that painting anywhere — grand trees in summer leaf, Constable's piled-up clouds, his black horses pulling their wooden cart through the ford; a never-ending summer's day in southern England, in 1821.

The farmhouse where the print hangs is not in England, but on the Hebridean island of Coll. The window looks over a ragged little bay of rock and seaweed, where a red boat is drawn up. A wire fence, repaired with driftwood, keeps the sheep from the shore. In a boggy place where a thin burn wanders down to the shore there is a stand of yellow flag iris, and a single willow bush, where a sedge warbler is singing.

Coll and its twin island Tiree lie at a northeast-southwest axis, off the west coast of Mull. Between them like a hyphen is the tiny island of Gunna. Coll is a low, sandy affair with no hills and few trees. Only a few miles wide, its heights are rough moor knuckled with bedrock, with lochans in the dips. The island is ringed with beaches of flawless sand, backed by huge dunes. Atlantic squalls pass over rapidly and the air smells of seaweed. The sea and its surf is never far away, a constant Atlantic soughing, a sense that the land is an interruption in a long conversation between water and sky.

The point is, when Constable packed up his easel at the end of that summer's day, what he would have heard as he walked home through the fields — indeed, what we could hear if we could step into his painting — would be the call of the corncrake. A corncrake is a brown bird, a kind of rail, not ten inches tall, which prefers to remain unseen in tall damp grass. Its call — you'd hardly call it a song — is two joined notes, like a rasping telephone. *Crex Crex* is the bird's Latin name, a perfect piece of onomatopoeia. *Crex-crex*, it goes, *crex-crex.*

Perhaps, as he strolled home, Constable had a bit of fun trying to pinpoint the sound in the long grass. Perhaps he thought nothing of it, the corncrake being such a commonplace. "Heard in every vale," as John Clare said in his poem. The vales of Northamptonshire, the New Town of Edinburgh, in Robert Burns's Ayrshire, it was recorded in every county in the land from Cornwall to Shetland. In the last century, though, it has been utterly eliminated from the mainland, and if you'd like to hear or even see this skulking little bird of the meadow you must sail to the Hebrides.

Saturday night on Coll. Nowadays the human population is about 160, incomers mostly — much the same as the number of corncrakes. I don't know how many of them turned up for the disco; that was last night. Monday is the African drumming group, but there are other diversions. It's eleven at night. Elsewhere people are doubtless getting ready to go out clubbing, but I'm pulling on wellies and a jacket. It's not quite dark and a Land-Rover has pulled up at the side of the guesthouse.

The Land-Rover, a smart new example of corporate sponsorship, is driven by Sarah Money, warden of the RSPB reserve on Coll. Her reserve is managed especially for corncrakes, and Sarah's work, late on this Saturday night, is to go out into the fields to census — that is, count — these little brown birds. "Medium-sized brown birds, please," Sarah says.

When we're ready, Sarah, a fit woman in her thirties, jolts

the vehicle down onto the beach and drives hard across the sand for a mile and a half. There is no road to the guesthouse. Above the engine she's saying that you have to keep a good speed. Too slow, you'll sink into the sand. She's telling a yarn of a man who did just that — got his Land-Rover stuck and went to fetch a tractor to pull it out. That got stuck as well, and then the tide came in and he lost both. Then we're bouncing off the beach again, and wind on a track through the dunes until Sarah stops the Land-Rover and winds down the window to listen. Satisfied, she cuts the engine. We jump down, and in the dark and the breeze open a gate and, by torchlight, enter a field.

Corncrake. Landrail. King of the Quail, the croaking one of the cornsheaf, the nutty noisemaker, the quailie, the weet-my-fit.

"Hear them?" she whispers, and I nod.

What does it sound like? Like someone grating a nutmeg, perhaps. Or a prisoner working toward his escape with a nail-file. *Crex-crex, crex-crex.* We move forward a few paces at a time. Now and again Sarah stops and tilts her head. She wears her hair back in a ponytail and sports two or three small earrings, and when she stops to listen she reminds me of a thrush on a lawn. She cups her hands behind her ears, because it's almost impossble to tell where exactly the sound is coming from. It's obviously on the ground — you'd swear it was right under your feet, but it seems to jump and flit ahead. We walk on carefully, speaking in whispers until we've crossed the whole field, but the sound heard so clearly from the gate is still, somehow, ahead of us.

It's unchancy. Fairy music is said to do this; to lead a man on in his confusion and drunkenness, to start, then stop, then begin again from another place, ever luring him on. This was not a beautiful music, it has to be said; hardly the art of the fairies. Mind you, it could be a goblin carpenter, sawing away at his little workbench, if you'd had a few too many at the island disco and were of fanciful mind.

Again Sarah stops and listens; she explains she's trying to tell whether we're hearing two different corncrakes, or just one who's using a rocky outcrop as a sounding board to give his call a bit of reverb and so steal a march on his rivals. Only males call like this; nocturnal lovers, they're trying to attract a mate. He keeps it up all night, every second or so. Now we're definitely close to the bird, the sound's coming from a patch of cow parsley at our feet, and at such close quarters it's a much lower, slower sound, a real smoky bar room rasp. *Crex-crex, crex-crex,* he goes, more Tom Waits than Tom Jones, but hugely sexy to female corncrakes. Then we're too close, he cuts to silence, and there's only the breeze and seals singing from the shore. We look at one another, trying not to laugh.

> *We hear it in the weeding time*
> *When knee deep waves the corn.*
> *We hear it in the summer's prime*
> *Through meadows night and morn:*
>
> *And now I hear it in the grass*
> *That grows as sweet again*
> *And let a minute's notice pass*
> *And now tis in the grain.*
>
> *Tis like a fancy everywhere*
> *A sort of living doubt;*
> *We know tis something but it ne'er*
> *Will blab the secret out . . .*

So wrote John Clare.

The grim reaper came for the corncrake in the form of the mechanised mower. In the days of the scythe, when hay was long and cut later in the year, then heaped on slow-moving wains, the corncrake had long grasses to hide and breed in. The chicks would be fledged before the meadow was mown, and had plenty of time to escape the swinging blade. With mechanisation, however, and a shift toward earlier cutting for silage, corncrakes, eggs, fledglings and all have been slaughtered wholesale.

The corncrake has long been in relationship with humans, its fortunes have waxed and waned as our own farm practices changed. When prehistoric people cleared woodland and developed agriculture, the bird's range extended: corncrake bones have been discovered in Stone Age middens. Indeed, Mrs Beeton gives a recipe for roasted corncrake. You need four, and should serve them, if liked, with a nice bread sauce. But since Clare's "mowers on the meadow lea" were likewise banished before the machine, the corncrakes' range has been reduced to a few boggy meadows on the islands. They are the same islands, ironically, whose human populations suffered such decline as ideas on farming changed. But old mowing practices lingered longer in the Hebrides, the fields being too small for machines, so this is where the bird is making its last stand, and where conservation efforts are taking effect.

So Sarah and I are standing in a damp, dark field, listening to corncrakes on the pull. The females' job is to respond to this sound, choose a mate, inspect the several nests the male, in a fit of high optimism, has already prepared on the ground, select one and get laying. You don't see the females much — they keep purdah, hiding deep in the nettles or iris patches, raising one or maybe two broods of jet-black chicks. Once a male has mated a female, he'll stick around for only a short time, until she lays eggs, then he starts rasping again to secure another. The mother duly hatches the chicks, but less than a fortnight later she abandons the little brood to fend for themselves. At that age, they can't even fly and are easy prey to otters or buzzards, but their mother is off choosing a second mate, to raise another brood.

To our minds, this strategy has an air of desperation, of profligacy — raise lots of young against the onslaught. It's one we, as a species, are leaving behind. But Sarah says the corncrake's life is so perilous that the male we're hearing now may not be the one she counted here last year. He has doubtless perished. This may be his son, returned to the place of his birth, to fulfil his imperative and breed. So there he is, a tiny, urgent male rasping at our feet, and it gives Sarah and me the giggles.

At about two o'clock in the morning Sarah's satisfied and ready to go home to bed. By the light of the Land-Rover's lamp, she makes notes on a clipboard. The night's sally has brought her total of calling males to 73, which is on track to beat last year's record. Ten years ago, before this reserve was established with enclaves of long grasses and considerate mowing, there were but twenty, so 73 counts as success. The night is mild, a soft breeze blows from the sea. A mile inland a single light is shining in the window of a house. Maybe someone's sleepless, what with this incessant scratchy chorus all night long.

The next morning I stroll along the beach; the tide has washed away the Land-Rover's tracks. There's an oil drum, an oyster-catcher's nest and a long-dead dolphin. Behind the beach, on the huge sand dunes wild flowers are coming into bloom, bloody cranesbill, orchids like pink thumbs. From the end of the beach I follow a track inland until it passes the field where Sarah and I stood last night. Last night it seemed an unsettling place; now it's green and benign. Crouched in the grass like intelligent stones are half a dozen brown hares, and in the middle stands a scarecrow with a bucket for a head. But there, from deep in the growth at the field's far edge, comes that noise again: *crex-crex, crex-crex, crex-crex.*

By her house at the reserve, Sarah's flattening the grass with a strimmer; she's splattered with green gunk. She cuts the motor, invites me into the kitchen for coffee, and at a table piled with guides to flowers and bird reports she tells me she acquired her considerable knowledge of birds quickly, in only eight years, as an adult rather than as an obsessive adolescent. It was an extended visit to St Kilda which turned her interest. Knowing birds is like being fluent in a foreign language, or adept with a musical instrument. Though managing a bird reserve appears more like gardening or housewifery than the call of the wild, what with its careful planting and egg-counting, it still attracts few women. The postings can be hard on a family and a partner's needs, if indeed you have a family. If not, finding a partner in an out-of-the-way place can be difficult.

"Will you stay here?" I ask.

"Not forever. It would drive me mad."

Coll would be a heavenly place to be a child. There are beaches and boats, everyone knows you, it's the kind of place you leave your door open. If you're on the island, it's known. If you catch the ferry to the mainland, well, that's known about too. Should you have a mishap and require the air ambulance, a helicopter will have you in a Glasgow hospital in twenty minutes, by which time the island will have learned of your fate. A mere thirteen miles of single-track road separates "the unspoiled end" from "God's own country." There are local land feuds, a limited supply of fresh water, and no high school. In effect, the children leave home when they are an unfledged eleven, to travel as boarders to the secondary school in Oban. Higher education and jobs take them yet farther afield. It seems a price to pay for an apparently idyllic island life, to lose your children so young.

Corncrakes migrate. They arrive in April or May, by night. They fly reluctantly, by all accounts, low, with hunched wings. "Embarrassed," one field guide says, of their flying style. Sometimes they collide with power-lines and lighthouses. Then in September they leave again. From the Hebrides to southern Africa—it seems unbelievable. But then, folk believed unlikely things of the corncrake: that it vanished underground in winter, or changed into a moorhen or, if it flew at all, it hitched a ride on other birds. Or that it lies on its back when making its call, otherwise the sky would fall in. Where the birds winter is not exactly known—only one corncrake ringed in Scotland has ever been recovered, and that was in the Congo. They endure this epic migration, then lose themselves again in the long grass.

"It's good that we don't quite know," says Sarah. "Good that there is still some mystery in the world. And if we don't know, it suggests they go where there are no people, and that's better for the birds."

"And what do you do then, in the winter, on the reserve?" I ask, and Sarah says, with genuine enthusiasm, "Oh, we have the geese to look forward to. You know that day in October when you sense the year's turned? Then the geese come."

<hr/>

Not content with having heard several corncrakes by night, I want to see one. It's a species thing. As humans, we privilege sight; it confirms the other senses. I'd been told, "You don't see corncrakes if you're looking for them," but still, I'd feel short-changed if I didn't. The RSPB has established a "corncrake viewing bench" which is a grand name for a few slats of wood on the edge of a field. Sarah takes me there. Her task today is to survey lapwings' nests, because lapwings too are in decline, and she wants to find out why. "Might be otters — there's a nice conservation dilemma." She pulls on jacket and wellies, takes her clipboard and we set out for the fields.

The bench gives a view over the gentle downward slope of two lush meadows, which are divided by a wire fence and a row of telegraph poles carrying wires to a cottage three-quarters of a mile away. Wide borders at the fields' edges have been left to grow long, and cow parsley and grasses sway in the wind. The long grasses provide cover for corncrakes. In the marshy middle of the fields, waders nest. The fields are swathes of muted yellows and creams — buttercups, yellow rattle, cow parsley. The land dips, then rises. In the dip is a little open water, where reeds and flag iris grow, and a couple of greylag geese are idling there. It's not ideal weather for corncrake viewing. The sky's overcast and threatens squalls, the breeze is too fresh. A wind above three knots, and corncrakes don't like to come out. They don't like flying, don't much care for wind and rain, don't want to be seen in public — the kind of bird who'd want to be excused games. Not like these lapwings, hurling themselves down through the air trying to divert Sarah, who's investigating their nests.

I watch her stooping in the field like a gleaner. It looks like a life, a good job to hold, to be counting corncrakes by night, and checking lapwings' nests in a boggy field by day — beats being stuck in an office. She will tell you, however, that most of a warden's work is negotiating and compromising with people, rather than birds. Given the conditions, the birds will look after themselves. It's the tenant farmers and neighbours and visitors that take the management. To be eccentric landlord to some, and charming host to others; to keep smiling, even to those people whom you believe are fouling up the planet. She says there are people hostile to the very idea of conservation; who believe it's somehow anti-human and therefore unacceptable to devote a corner of a faraway field to the endangered corncrake, to let them raise a few chicks and then go.

I want to see a corncrake. So I sit on the bench and watch the lacy heads of cow parsley waft in the breeze. I'm thinking about corncrakes, as though thinking about them could summon one up. A glimpse is all I'll be granted — maybe a female darting from one patch of cover to another, or rival males so forgetting themselves as to have a quick squabble in public view. The corncrake has become a Hebridean bird, part of the Hebridean summer along with the blue windswept skies, the surf and rain, the wild flowers on the machair, the skylarks and the empty, cream-pale beaches. Its decline is doubtless bad for the corncrake, but there's an interesting side effect. In this age of supposed homogeneity and sameness where, as naturalist Richard Mabey put it, "the differences between native and stranger are fading," we have driven the birds away. Once-common species, like the corncrake, are becoming more localised, more specialised. But, as they do, it seems that people are learning a new identification with the birds of their patch. Mull makes much of its sea eagle, a species that was hunted to extinction, then reintroduced.

On Coll everyone knows about corncrakes — they're adopting them as their own, like the totems of Neolithic tribes. On Coll, it's corncrakes that are good for business. Summer visitors themselves, they beget others. Birdwatchers come especially — Sarah tells of an old lady who sat quiet and demure on this very viewing bench for an hour, two hours . . . then there was a whoop, and Sarah turned to see the old lady leaping around, punching the air like a footballer, just for a glimpe of an elusive brown bird. I sit on the bench, looking at the long grass, but it's beginning to rain, and though there are geese and lapwings and redshanks, a flock of noisy starlings, and a laverock rising, I see no corncrake. Maybe it's just as well. In Shetland they held it was very bad luck, actually to clap eyes on the thing.

When, later that day, I do see one, it's scuttering away from the wheels of the car. Like a miniature road-runner, a slender upright hen with hunched shoulders and strong, long pinkish legs, it squeezes under a wire fence, and with relief vanishes among the irises, even as I brake. It's the colour of slipware and looks, in that glimpse, like an elegant ceramic water jug suddenly come to life. That's that. I do not punch the air.

Corncrakes don't feature on Christmas cards, or sing after the rain. Their migration has none of the romance of swallows', though they cover the distance. They arrive in spring, but we've forgotten they are spring's heralds. They skulk in the grass like guilty things, hardly encouraging us to look to the skies. They offer us no metaphors about fidelity, or maternal dedication; they are just medium-sized brown birds. Nonetheless, I feel robbed — denied one of the sounds of summer, which all our forebears would have known, that irksome little *crex-crex*. Why conserve them, other than it being our moral duty to another life form on this earth? If there is no "clam'rin craik," no "noisy one of the rushes," it betokens something out of kilter with the larger ecosystem on which ultimately, in mysterious as-yet-undiscovered ways, we all depend.

That's what the ecologists and scientists will tell you. But there are things which cannot be said — not by scientists, anyway. Another person arrives at the viewing bench, not an old lady but a man in young middle age, a holiday-maker. We fall into conversation — he obviously knows his stuff about birds. He has a young family with him on the island and, while they're on the beach, he has slunk off for an hour in the hope of spotting a corncrake. So here he is, an Englishman of higher education with a professional job, a family, a cagoule and good binoculars.

"Can I ask why you like them? Corncrakes I mean."

"Well," he said. "They're like . . . little gods of the field, aren't they?"

I could have punched the air. If corncrakes are rare, animism is rarer still. Anyone can clear his throat and talk about biodiversity, but "Corncrakes . . . little gods of the field" will not get you published in ornithologists' journals. That's how I picture them now, however: standing chins up, open-beaked, like votive statues hidden in the grass.

When I nip in to thank Sarah before heading for the ferry she's in her customary work-gear, Barbour and wellies, and is on her way out to replace the battery in an electric fence. A farmer at the other end of the island has just phoned to report corncrakes on his land, thereby bringing her total of calling males on the island to 75, breaking last year's record, so Sarah's pleased — though their future, to paraphrase John Clare, is still "a sort of living doubt."

At Arinagour, where the ferry docks, are a few white cottages, a shop, a hotel. There is also a pottery where you can buy a souvenir ceramic corncrake to take back to the mainland. There's talk of reintroducing real corncrakes to England, so it might again *crex* through Constable's Dedham Vale. Till then the mainland's a diminished place; a thousand miles of country without one little god in its fields.

Fever

Under the gutter of our house are many cobwebs, each attached at a slightly different angle to the wall. It's an east-facing wall, so on sunny mornings the cobwebs are alight.

The cobwebs made me think of ears, or those satellite dishes attuned to every different nuance of the distant universe. One cobweb after another — a whole quarter of cobwebs, like an Eastern bazaar with all the cobblers, all the spice-sellers, all the drapers together in their own alleys. The biggest web measured about a hand-span and a half, a pianist's hand-span. I wondered if all the spiders were related, a family group.

In the bedroom in the house behind me, my husband was ill and rapidly becoming worse. He'd sustained a temperature of forty degrees for four days now, too hot even to sweat. Rather, he sweated at night and slumbered, radiantly hot, by day. In the hours when he slept, and when the children were at school or nursery, a rare, spacious, elegant air came over the house. I sat on the step — you enter our house on the upper floor, via an outside staircase — in the late summer sun and noticed the bright cobwebs under the gutter. I noticed acutely the cobwebs and the tiny flies adrift in the sunny morning air, and remember thinking that some of the flies would surely find their way into the cobwebs. I noticed, or rather felt, the sunlight intensifying and fading on the stone wall behind me as clouds passed.

Sunlight and cobwebs, and when I went in and put my head round the bedroom door to check on Phil, I watched for a moment the light refracted by our old window, which formed a silent rippling pond on the bedroom ceiling.

He was hot, half-asleep, his back turned to me. He asked only for more water. His skin had a grey-yellow pallor. The doctor had examined him, then stood looking at Phil in silence for a long moment, then shaken his head. We knew from tests urgently processed that Phils's blood was destroying itself. "We've got to get to the bottom of this," the doctor said.

When the phone rang, I jumped. It was our GP, giving instructions about the hospital, the number of a ward, the name of a professor. I went back indoors to help Phil get ready and make arrangements to have the children collected after school.

Neither of us had ever been to the hospital before. It was more like an international airport. We entered a shopping mall, with opticians and hairdressers and cafés. As in an airport, destination boards were suspended over our heads and arrows pointed to wide corridors that led to Assisted Conception, School of Anaesthesia, Phlebotomy Unit, Haematology. Slowly we walked down one of these corridors, a distance of perhaps half the length of our garden, until Phil collapsed. I brought a wheelchair from the front desk and valiantly we found our way to where we had been sent.

In a small consulting room, screened from the door by a half-drawn curtain, the senior nurse explained that, although this ward was part of the oncology unit, not everyone here had cancer. She brought a fan into the room, plugged it in, switched it on. We were learning new words: "pyrexic." Phil lay back on the narrow bed. The door opened often as junior doctors and nurses entered, opened drawers and plastic tubs and took away phials and needles, tubes and latex gloves. Once a junior doctor came and took several samples of Phil's blood.

The senior doctor was a brisk woman. She was crisply dressed, in a blouse, tailored hound's-tooth skirt, Italian shoes. Slowly Phil sat up, and pulled off his T-shirt. Already his body had lost some of his carpenter's muscle tone and taken on a submissive slump. Leaning across the bed behind him, the doctor placed her stethoscope at precise points on Phil's back, and began to listen. As she listened, she created around herself a screen of privacy. Her eyes disengaged. She folded herself into the stethoscope, in toward Phil's back, attending to the sound as a musician might. Then she began concentrating on an area midway down his right side. She was tracking something within his body, moving the stethoscope an inch to the left, an inch to the right then back again, as if comparing two notes. Suddenly she was satisfied, and leaned back, tugging the stethoscope out of her ears.

I drove home alone, back across the long bridge over the Tay. The tide was out, exposing long sandbanks. I took the minor road, the scenic route high above the shining water. Soon it would be time to collect the kids, and explain to them why their father had vanished. But first I went out into the garden. Our garden is long and thin. Phil planted a beech hedge along its length three years ago, which has filled out from spindly saplings into a thickness of bright green. I passed the young rowan tree. My paces took me to the door of the larch shed he built last summer. It has stained-glass windows and a shingle roof, and above its door he hung a plaque with a green man with fronds of plum tree issuing from the mouth. Beyond the shed is the plum orchard; beyond that, three old apple trees, one with a half-finished tree-house he was building before he fell ill.

The alveoli, we're told, if they were unpacked from our lungs and spread out, would cover the area of a tennis court, 78 feet by 27. Or from the wall to the hedge breadthwise, and the bench to the shed longways. An area the mellow sun was now casting with long afternoon shadows. I stood with my back to the shed and surveyed the area, tried to imagine, what? What are we to imagine, the breathing area of our lungs, the 600 million alveoli? Spread out like what? Tarpaulin? Frost? A fine, fine cobweb, exchanging gases with the open air? And what of our nerves? There are hundreds of miles of neurones in our brains. I tried to imagine it, all that nerve, all that awareness and alertness spread out around me. All that listening.

That night, at bedtime, I took our son's *Child's World Encyclopaedia* and showed the kids pictures of lungs, of blood, of nerves. They never asked if their dad might die. Maybe it never occurred to them that people who fall ill may die.

The X-ray gives an external image of something we carry within ourselves. An image we have to draw out of ourselves, that we might see it in front of our eyes, and so take it within ourselves again. Out of the lungs and into the brain. From Phil's hospital bed we could see the lightbox where the doctors examine X-rays. There was a shape, a shadow on the right lung. Two doctors in white coats stood side by side pointing to it. One glanced back over her shoulder at us. This was his pneumonia, this was what the examining doctor could hear as she listened so intently. I recalled her professional satisfaction: "I would be very interested to see this gentleman's chest X-ray."

The image of the disease, though, is an image of the way things were some time ago. Pneumonia leaves a scar behind, then moves on. The shadow we can see on the X-ray from deep within our bodies, like the images our telescopes receive from the distant universe, shows us an image of something already in the past.

But pneumonia, nowadays, is easily dealt with. Phil's real problem was that it had caused him to produce antibodies which were wreaking havoc on his own red blood cells. His red blood count was already half what it should be, and still falling. That's why he had been sent to this ward, haematology. Many samples had been taken. Somewhere in a laboratory, a smear of his blood was cooling on a slab. Perhaps even now someone was attending to it, focusing through the lenses of a microscope.

On the ward, no one was sitting up. There was a man with sickle-cell anaemia; all I could see of him were his slim black feet sticking out from the sheet. Two of the other men were bald, perhaps as a result of chemotherapy. A third man slept most of the time with his back turned to his wife, who sat at his bedside, reading a paperback. When the man died, without warning, the next day, Phil told me she'd cried, "Don't leave me! Don't leave me!"

When my mother was a child, during the Second World War, what few antibiotics could be made were sent to the Front. When she contracted pneumonia, none were available. She was four, an only child. She told me this story perhaps three times. She told it me again quite recently, when my own child, her grandson, himself turned four. We were in the café of the Queen Street Gallery in Edinburgh, which was conveniently close to the offices of the firm of solicitors where she worked. My mother was her stylish, professional self. But we were talking about pneumonia and wartime. At that last telling, I understood. I had by then stood at the doorway of a child's room, leaned over a cot and listened for the small, blessed exchange of air in their new lungs.

My mother lived with her mother in a tenement flat; her father was away at the war. The flat had a sink under the window and a bed in the kitchen recess, and it smelled of coal. Even into the 1960s, when I was taken there as child to visit my nana, the window in the common stair remained painted in blackout, and the landing was lit by gas. There was no bathroom, of course, just a toilet down at the turn of the stair. Two households shared the one lavatory.

When my mother fell ill, a doctor was called, and my mother always told me the same two things about the doctor — one, that he never sent a bill, and two, that he never entered the room. Not from snobbery or fear of contagion; it was how he made his diagnosis, how he gauged the severity of her disease. She remembers almost sixty years on how the doctor stood in the door listening to her labouring breath, then turned heel to arrange for an ambulance. For three weeks she lay in the adult ward for chest diseases, in a bed next to the window. The hospital was some distance from town, but her mother and grandmother walked out to see her every day. Twice they were summoned during the night because the girl wasn't expected to live till dawn.

What she remembers of the hospital was that her mother and grandmother were not allowed to see her. Rather, she was not allowed to see them. A screen or curtain was pulled round the bed and her visitors were hidden behind it. Except: she could see their shoes. The little girl knew her mother and granny were there listening, by those sturdy, wartime shoes showing below the screen. When she was on the mend and allowed to sit outside in the fresh air, the nurses dressed her up in their starched cuffs and hats. This is what she remembers. She couldn't see her mother because the nurses feared a display of emotion, a sudden fit of crying, would overload her already strained heart and lungs and would cost her her life. Emotional control as survival mechanism is what I, as her daughter, think of as her legacy from that disease. It never occurred to me that Phil might have pneumonia because he was silent, and I knew my mother's story so well, about the doctor standing in the doorway, listening to her hauling breath.

The next day, I took the children in to visit their dad, but removed them again soon. Some of the ambulatory patients were wandering around hooked up to a vertical web of tubing which trundled along beside them on wheels, as if their own circulatory systems were external to them. Blood and saline dripped slowly through tubes and gauges into limp arms. I was scared that the kids, who were already bored with their father, and who were sliding around the floor, might cause one of these people and their apparatus-on-wheels to trip over in a horrible tangle of blood and tubing and frail pyjamaed bodies.

On the way out again, the children wanted to show me a bird. We were walking along the wide corridor that would take us back to the shopping mall and covered walkway to the car park. There were windows that overlooked a flat asphalt roof, and on the roof was a starling, lying on its back.

"It's dead! Look, mummy! It's dead!"

"No, it isn't! Mummy, look! It's moving its legs! But it will soon be dead."

I pulled them away from the window and past the door to the School of Anaesthesia, toward the car.

～

"Whom do you pray to?" A friend asked me, once.

"No one," I replied. "Absolutely nothing."

We were eating fish and chips. I never pray. Why should one pray? What do you do? Supplicate? Haggle? Haggle with God?

Maybe if my child was lying mortally ill behind a screen, I'd pray, but it would be self-conscious. Hope is an appalling feeling. We pray, I guess, to displace for a moment the crush of hope. I couldn't have discussed this with my friend over our chips, but I carried this question around with me for a while. Really I carried it around until Phil was so ill, then berated myself for not praying. Could I explain to Phil that — though there was a time, maybe twenty-four hours, when I genuinely believed his life to be in danger — I had not prayed? But I had noticed, more than noticed, the cobwebs, and the shoaling light, and the way the doctor listened, and the flecked tweed of her skirt, and the speckled bird and the sickle-cell man's slim feet. Isn't that a kind of prayer? The care and maintenance of the web of our noticing, the paying heed?

"What about you?" I asked. "Who do you pray to?"

He took another chip and shrugged. "Dunno. But she's female. Great Mother, or something."

～

We went for a walk up Ormiston Hill, the children and me, behind our town. The land rises steeply in a series of terraces. It's rough grazing with banks of whin. The kids, in their blue wellies, struggled along well through the long grass. We could see the town below us. "There's Ben's house!" they said. "There's the school!" The park, the river — almost the whole compass of their lives. Downriver, where the water widens yet more, we could see Dundee where their father was in hospital. The Firth of Tay is wide here. The tide's inhalations and exhalations move vast tonnages of water. Water retreats and exposes sandbanks.

Upstream the river folds itself into the hills. It pulls into itself the light of the sky, moves through the land like a bright coil. We ate some brambles. We climbed a five-bar gate, noted the ditch which is all that remains of an Iron Age fort built on the hilltop, then passed through the wicket gate onto the summit. I tried to show them how to treat the jaggy whin. "Just go, don't be scared. Just barge into it. It won't hurt half as much as you think. It's your own fear that's stopping you." But they baulked and demanded to be lifted over.

At the summit I sat and looked at the countryside while the kids, having demanded the biscuits we'd brought, scrambled on the summit cairn. The hill's not high, only a thousand feet or so, but the reaches of land around it are wide. We could see plantation forest and mountains to the west, farmland and lochs to the south and east. A visitor from Texas once told us our landscape was human-scale. The wind packed itself into our lungs and hair.

Some of the rocks on the cairn were loose, and Duncan rolled one in his scrambling, disturbing a long- legged spider. Duncan hesitated for half a moment, then, deliberately, before I could stop him, he rolled the stone and then lifted it again. The spider was still alive, but three of its legs were crushed against the stone. With the other five it scrambled and scrambled on empty air.

The nurse who came to scoosh the syringe full of saline and antibiotics into the little faucet in Phil's wrist had done this task so often she barely needed to look. The antibiotics were already having an effect, killing the bacteria wholesale. She was talking amiably about books, about what Phil was reading. He was well enough to read, now. She herself had just finished *Captain Corelli's Mandolin*. She looked back over her shoulder, laughing with the jolly tea lady as she scooshed the big syringe.

Attend! I wanted to say to her, though she hardly needed to. Here, I'll do it. I'll kill the infection. I'll do it with attention. Prayerfully, if you like.

The bed where the woman had read her paperback and the man had died was occupied again. The thin man with sickle-cell had been visited by his granddaughter, but she was only small and had to be taken away screaming from the sacs of blood and tubes and hairless people and X-rays and needles.

We went, en famille, to collect Phil on the Sunday. Six days' intravenous antibiotics had the infection on the run. His red blood count was rising. He'd had, he was told, cold agglutinin disease. We walked Phil slowly along the corridor that would lead to the shopping mall, the hospital doors, back into the air of the outside world. The kids skipped about, demanding attention he wasn't yet well enough to give. As we passed the window, they said, "Daddy, we've got something to show you. Look!"

"What is it?"

"A dead bird!"

Its chest cavity was burst open. Carrion crows or something had eaten away at the flesh of its breast, its ribs, its lungs.

"You did well," I said to my mother, "to survive that pneumonia, just a bairn and no antibiotics." She nodded.

"I can still remember the smell of the poultices. I was so weak, they had to bring me home in a baby's pram."

And if they'd had to bring her home in a box, none of this would have happened. Her life would not have been lived, nor then my sister's, nor my brother's, nor my own, nor those of my brother's daughters, nor my own daughter's, nor my son's.

It's unimaginable: you can't think yourself out of the world, as has been noted before. When we imagine being dead, it's an oxymoron, isn't it?

Writing this, I'd wanted to look again at the cobwebs. I hadn't noticed them with such intensity since. Not the spider webs nor anything else. I went to the door and looked up at the gutter, but the webs were hard to make out in the flat afternoon light. I could see, though, that they were tattered and hung with fire-weed seeds. We'd had our first frosts. Perhaps the spiders were hibernating. Do spiders hibernate? I went indoors and looked them up in my own encyclopaedia. The entry had been written by someone obviously enchanted by spiders, someone who must have spent hours watching, noticing, attending to spiders, and their lives of exquisite loneliness. The young hatch and then disperse "by climbing onto a vantage point, spinning a silk thread and waiting for the wind to catch it and whisk them away."

Markings

At the far side of the field was a long mound, the shape of a loaf. The field was a freshly mown green, but because the grasses on the mound had been left undisturbed — it was dun-coloured. The mound wasn't high, only twelve feet or so, and a single tree grew from its back. Behind it, shaded by oaks and birches, the river flowed.

A ghost of a trail, a mere suggestion, led across the field and up onto the mound and petered out beside an exposed area of bedrock, the size of a tabletop. Grasses, heavy with seed, had flopped over the exposed rock like hair across a brow, so I knelt and swept them aside.

Even so, the carvings were difficult to see at first, they were so old and weatherworn. A wintery, shadow-casting sun would have helped, or a recent shower, which would have filled each with a little water. They were depressions, rather than designs, and not deep — you could lay your fingers in, as you would into a jar of face cream, though the rock was rough and grainy to touch. There were more than forty carvings on this tabletop alone, and there were four or five such exposed areas on the eastward-facing side of the mound, all likewise covered with cup marks.

Cup marks, they may be called, or cup-and-ring marks, but cups and rings are safe, domestic things and these marks didn't seem homely. Rather they were strewn across the rockface like a bad case of acne, urgent and slightly worrying. I didn't know what to think of them, and in truth felt a bit daft, hunkering in a field like this, so I made the obligatory musings about the Neolithic hand which had carved them thousands of years ago, wondered what they had been for, inscribed for. What they meant, if indeed "meant" was quite the right word. The carvings themselves offered no clue, but lay mute in the morning sunshine. So, for want of anything better to do, I laid a page of my notebook over one of the carvings and traced it. On the rock, they look almost cosmological. On my page, though, it looked like a fried egg.

The sun, it was early August, was intense. The cup marks had been a digression, something spotted on the Ordnance Survey map, and I feared if I tarried much longer, it would be too hot to slog up to my intended destination higher in the hills. So I made my way back to the road, passed a farm with big metal barns, found the track given on the map, which, in a series of switchbacks up through bracken-covered slopes, climbed several hundred feet up onto the hills. An hour's walking later I was looking down on a grove of trees that marked the river's course through the glen, its flat, yellow mown meadows and the mound with the cup-marked stones. The high hills that closed off the top of the glen had that concussed look they take in the heat, and it was hard going, on and up. Twice a lizard darted from my foot, but few birds moved. Only a few puffy clouds drifted overhead, a few sheep grazed among bracken.

At length the track narrowed to a mere sheep path, then contoured round the hillside and led into a ravine where a burn cascaded down, over rocks. Walking upstream, I had my back to the lower valley now, and was heading into the hills. Beside the water grew a single tree, an old silver birch, and two moths were dancing beside it. At my approach, they flattened themselves against the bark of the tree. Had I not seen them moving together, I would never have noticed them now.

Then it was a matter of crossing the burn by jumping boulder to boulder before being conducted up and out of the steep ravine, and then the landscape changed. Indeed, I glanced back, but I'd reached that liminal, slightly unnerving point in any hill walk where, because of some fold in the land, you can no longer see the place you started out from. I'm not used to being in the hills alone. The lower valley — a thousand feet below, with its trees and cup-marked stones — had been withdrawn, and heather and hills put in its place. Hills surrounded me. Not high, not majestic, but rounded and in their summer green. There were no trees here, and no sound now of running water. In hot silence, I walked another short distance up onto a slight ridge, and from there could see the place I'd come looking for.

Silent as a stage, lying back northwards for a short mile, was a perfect high glen, in browns and subtle greens. A hanging valley, held, as it were, in the arms of its surrounding hills. It had been a steep climb up, but now the land relaxed, levelled. Through the middle of this high valley the river knew no urgency. It moved in wide, slow meanders, like a rope played out. From my vantage point, on a slight rise somewhat higher than the valley floor, the whole scene looked like a painting. No, a photograph.

What came to mind, oddly, were those early photographs of American Indian encampments, of tepees and horses beside a river. It must have been the stillness, and the muted, near sepia tones of the heather and green grass, and a sense of balanced composition. Of course there were no tepees — well, not exactly, and no wind — that's what made me think of pictures. In the hills there is almost always some movement of air, at least a breeze, but today the air held a calm, attentive heat.

Where the river ran over stones, it glinted. In its slower places, it held a touch of blue, borrowed from the sky. Its little flood plains, the places contained within its meanders, were a fresh, springlike green. Other than the water, the land was quite still. Above the hills, a buzzard drifted into sight, hung against the blue for a moment, then slid away. To east and to west heather moor ran away, a purplish brown, and the air smelled dry, herby. Scattered in among the heather were piles of grey stones, left behind, I supposed, by a retreating glacier a long time ago. At its northern border, the glen was closed by a higher rim, like a shallow bowl. Beyond this glen, up toward the watershed were glimpses of farther hillsides in a come-hither shade of sunny green. But they were far away. This graceful little glen, confined and complete, had that sense you find in quiet landscapes, of great age youthfully borne.

But then, as I was standing there, thinking these grand thoughts, something in the glen moved and my heart lurched. I took it at first for a man, a lone hillwalker or a shepherd. A man's presence wouldn't have surprised me much. A lone woman's would. My first mothlike instinct — don't know why — was to hide myself, but I was standing on the skyline, obvious to anyone below. Instead I lifted the binoculars and focused — but it was only a cow, a sleek grey cow, paddling in the river. I lowered the glasses and sat down on a rock.

The thing was, sudden movements or no, I was nervous because confounded. As I say, I was unaccustomed to being out in the hills on my own and felt a bit vulnerable, but I'd come looking for something in particular and could not see it. The lovely valley lay before me, but there was nothing to be seen. Pulling the map out of my rucksack, I checked again. Was this the wrong glen entirely? But there was the path, the deep cleugh where the river spilled down. I could lay my own thumb over the map's thumbprint of contour lines: tight for the ravine, then the 300-metre line softening and spacing out into this valley. But the map said shielings. It was insistent — shielings, shielings, and showed the glen crowded with tiny brown squares. With the map on my knee, I surveyed the real glen in front of me like a broad dish, scanned it west to east: from the summits, their side-slopes, the heather and piles of stones, the shining river, the farther, distant hills. There was nothing resembling a shieling to be seen.

The piles of stones. Somehow the cow in her river had helped my brain adjust to the scale. The fitful little path — I was beginning to expect its appearance when needed — was again under my feet, so I stood, shouldered my rucksack and walked on.

The path — possibly a very old path indeed — led on through knee-deep heather, down a slope, across a rivulet and upwards toward a green knoll. Green, because it was covered not in heather but in short, bright turf. On top of this knoll was a gable-end. This had been my piles of stones. It was a small dry-stone humble thing, no taller than myself, and as thick as my arm is long. In fact, there were two small gables, joined by low, very tumbledown walls. The stones — just fieldstones, gathered from around here — had been hefted into place by hand, and were now all fallen down, and thick with lichen and soft moss, and tufts of fleece from sheep who had found shelter there from the wind. The little building had no roof at all, in fact it was nothing but a rough rectangle of stones, enclosing a plot of moor grass. A long time had passed since it was last used and now it was slowly sinking back into the earth.

A gap in the wall showed where the door had once been, so I entered, and as I did so found myself nodding an acknowledgment to the woman of the house, which was silly really. Of course there was no-one there. The interior was very small, maybe ten or twelve feet from one end to the other; it was just a little plain ruin, in an empty glen.

The view was lovely, though. Because this hut lay a little higher on the hillside, in rather queenly dignity on top of its green knoll, the whole, photograph-like scene was laid silently in front of me. Not a great vista of peaks and ridges, but a contained place, almost domestic and serene. Now my eye was in, I could see the other shielings. The green knolls were a giveaway, and I counted — as the map had suggested — first one, then another humble little hut, until there were fourteen, and a little field system too, just a few undulations on the ground. There were seven or eight huts straggling along the riverside, forming not a street exactly, they were too spaced out, but the suggestion of one, of neighbourliness.

I leaned back into the sunny inner corner and, wondering when a woman had last eaten a meal in this little shelter, took out my sandwiches and flask. Her meal might have been bannocks and whey, I suppose. Then, having eaten, I turned my face to the sun, and closed my eyes.

Shielings, and shieling grounds, were the high summer pastures, the places where the cattle were driven to graze on fresh grass for the few weeks at the top of the year. The word refers to both the grounds and the shelters the people built for themselves for the duration. It was an old, old system, this transhumance. The people who had craved the cups and rings probably knew this place as good grazing; maybe that's why they stayed. It persisted a long time. Recently, I met a Hebridean man, just turned into his sixties. An engineer who'd worked all over the world, a man interested in art and jazz, he told me he'd been carried as a baby to the shielings in a creel on his granny's back. But here, in the Central Highlands, the practice had died out at the time of the Improvements, in the latter half of the eighteenth century.

The top of the year, the time of ease and plenty. The people would come up from the farmsteads below around the beginning of July — "the girls went laughing up the glen" as the poem says — and return at harvest time. Up here they made milk, butter and cheese, and it was women's work. What a loss that seems now: a time when women were guaranteed a place in the wider landscape, our own place in the hills. I'd taken that grey cow for a man. The presence in this valley of another woman, as I say, would have surprised me.

I dozed in the sun until wakened by the tiniest movement. A wren had flown from a cranny in the gable and plucked a crane fly out of the air. With the insect wriggling in its beak, it jinked back in between the stones. I roused myself to move on.

Because the day was so warm, and would be long, and this high valley so removed from the world and pleasing, it became a sort of task to visit each of the old shielings door to door, like an itinerant pedlar. The little path linked them, knoll to green knoll, and each was hailing distance from the next. But there was no-one there, not a man, not a woman or child; only that single grey cow, and two or three of her kind farther up on the hillside. One day soon, I dare say, someone would come up from the big farm in the valley to round them up, and bring them down for the winter, and that would be that for another year.

The riverside ground was damp, and fresh green grass grew on little flood plains. There was a ring of stones there, perhaps a fank — a pen — for calves, and some structures so old they were mere humps of thick moss. The shieling huts maintained their silent presence in the valley. Following the river upstream, I paused to creep inside first one, then the next.

Though they were all built of the same harsh, angular stone, each was slightly different. This one was close to the river — its occupants would have had a plentiful water supply — and it had a boulder of shining quartz by its door, which reflected the sun. Some huts had been divided into two tiny rooms, and where the inner partition wall was still intact the doorway was so low I'd to leave my little rucksack at the door and creep through on hands and knees. Some of the huts had stone recesses built into their walls, cool places to stand butter or cheese. Every hut, though, had taken on its own slow accretions of lichen, and moss with tiny scarlet beads, and stone had slipped from stone.

They were never meant to be permanent, always would have been the subject of running repairs and re-building. What was more lasting, a stronger mark on the landscape of the glen, were the green knolls each hut had created around itself. I don't know the reason for this; perhaps a long fertilisation and trampling by tethered calves, or urine. Whatever it was, it has lasted to this day. Two centuries on, the shieling huts were ruins but the grass still remembered to be green.

Women and children, youngsters giving each other the eye. The glen would have smelled of dung, of peat smoke. Perhaps they brought hens up, too, as well as the cattle. It would not have been silent. Men finding some excuse to wander up from the farms below. With no dour sermonising minister, warm days, light summer nights. A local woman said to me later, "Oh, there are so many songs in Gaelic about the shielings!"

From hut to hut I wandered, higher up the glen, and all day encountered no one else, not a man, not a woman or child, although it was warm, and the schools were on holiday, and in the nearest town, at the top of the loch, a mere four miles away as the crow flies, was a holiday resort. Its caravan site was crowded and the hostel full of hill-walkers.

The long school summer holiday — surely a remnant of our pastoral days, a last lingering trace of transhumance, when the women and children would take to the hills, driving the cattle before them. And what is a caravan, if not a shieling hut on wheels? But, as I say, if you stay off the summits, you can go all day without meeting another adult. And a child in the hills? Never.

In the afternoon I walked beyond the enclosure of the shieling grounds and farther up to the watershed. They're difficult places to negotiate, watersheds. The ground's choppy with peat hags and sudden lips, where rain and snow-melt draining down from the higher hills dither and slouch and form sullen pools, like teenagers at a bus stop, before finding their direction. Back toward its source, the river was a dark vein. A dipper, startled from its solitary concerns, took off low and fast over the moor. By now the sky was clouding over, and it was tempting to walk farther, down into the next valley, because the air was cooler now. The green knolls of yet more abandoned shielings lay higher in side-valleys.

From cup-marked stones to abandoned shielings; it seemed in one day, and by accident, I'd found the marks of the opening, and the closure, of life lived directly on the land. It startled me when I looked again at my notebook. There, on one page, was the fried-egg tracing, and on the very next page a few notes on those huts, abandoned a couple of centuries ago. Four or five thousand years of human subsistence, a few marks on a piece of paper.

Sometimes you hear this land described as "natural" or

"wild" — "wilderness," even — and though there are tracts of Scotland north and west of here, where few people live, "wilderness" seems an affront to those many generations who took their living on that land. Whether their departure was forced or whether that way of life just fell into abeyance, they left such subtle marks. And what's natural? We're having to replant the forests we cleared, there's even talk of reintroducing that natural predator, the wolf.

The watershed was only halfway to the summits of the biggest hills, but already the air had an autumnal hint. Without the bright sun, the want of trees gave the land a honed, wintery look. Fifteen hundred feet below, at the place of the cupmarked stones, the trees were in piled-up summer plenitude, but at the shieling grounds change was in the air. They'd have been packing up their pots and pans, taking down the roof timbers and driving the cattle downhill again for another year. Summer over, all hands were needed for the harvest.

I walked back down, through that graceful — I almost said girlish — glen, with its river and green grass, its mossy ruins sinking back into the earth, its sense of serene abandonment. Down in the ravine was the single silver birch. I stopped there to drink, and wash my face in the burn, but though I looked for the two dancing moths they were nowhere to be seen.

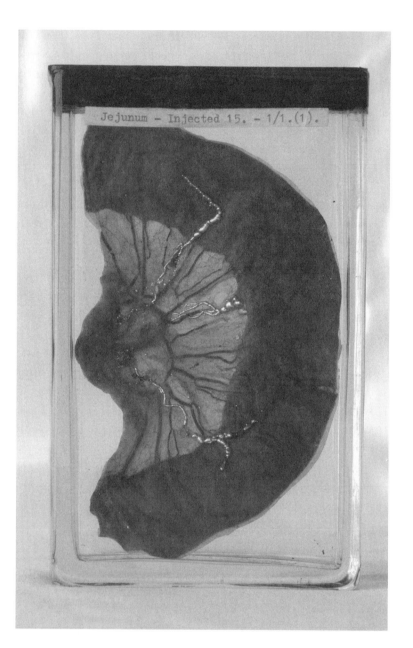

Jejunum – Injected 15. – 1/1.(1).

Surgeons' Hall

The arm hangs relaxed, the fingers of the hand curled slightly in toward the palm — a habit, they say, which links us to our ancestral apes. Because of the hair, I think it is a man's arm and it has been severed just below the elbow. It startled me. I'd been looking at something else, but then, having been invited to gaze at the severed arm, I kneel on the polished wooden floor and do so. It's held very still in a rectangular glass jar. You could read its fortune, the lifeline and heartline are so clear and the fingernails are just too long. Perhaps they kept growing after death.

The whole is stained a faint rust-red. The flesh of the forearm, though, is corroded and blotched with cancerous growths. Stuck to the jar is a label which has been typed unevenly on an obsolete machine. It reads, tersely, "Paraffin worker's arm. 1936."

The jar containing the arm stands silently on a white shelf, one in a row of other jars. Above it are more white shelves, holding more glass jars, and within the jars more specimens. There is a whole hall of them, with an upper gallery too, where further shelves hold further objects suspended in sealed jars. The hall is illuminated by a soft daylight, which falls evenly from frosted glass rooflights and the windows, which are screened by pale blinds. Beyond the windows is a world, where it is autumn. Almost, one can hear the city traffic, occasionally a shout or a door closing elsewhere in the college building. Within the hall, though, the rows and rows of jars know no season, no traffic nor haste.

—————

The chemical intervention which arrests the natural processes of decay is called "fixing." Once fixed, a specimen can be kept for a long time. The oldest here have been fixed in their jars for two hundred years, and they are displayed in a place of special privilege. They stand up in the gallery, facing the hall's main doors. Within those jars, preserved in fluids which are viscous and nicotine-coloured are objects which could be fruits, but you know in your heart they are not.

Each of the bays on the main floor of the Playfair Hall is given to a particular body part or type of ailment. Thus the specimens taken from cancerous breasts oppose, as though in a shy dance, those from cancerous testicles. A label gives the condition, the date, and the name of the doctor who donated the specimen. The blood colours are all leached away and the objects reduced to pallid shades of beige. Here, says the typed label, is a breast with Paget's disease. Suspended in its solution the object re-sembles not a woman's breast, or even part of a breast. It looks like a mango stone. A few steps away are jars containing parts of men's testes. In one — the thick glass magnifies the sample slightly, and a few pubic hairs still issue from the skin — layer after layer of skin and subcutaneous tissue have been neatly cut through to reveal a tumour. The layers the scalpel has pared away are so thin and finely graded in colour, they resemble the bands in polished agate. In another jar are pebbles so smooth and round you'd be happy to pick them up on a beach and keep them in your pocket, but these are displayed within a urinary tract. There is a pale slice of kidney. The label, clattered out on that same machine, reads "war gas inhalation."

For two, perhaps three, hours, I have been gazing in silence at the objects in jars, privileged to be alone, moving from shelf to shelf in the calm light. The shelves are low; to examine the specimens you have often to bend down or kneel, as you do with a child who has cut his knee. Unless you have a professional interest, it's possible that the only bodies you've been intimate with, have scrutinised, have been the bodies of lovers or children. The act of unhurried, unmediated examination has hitherto been an act of love. Perhaps as a consequence, or perhaps because given the opportunity we do indeed feel for all of suffering humanity, a stranger's arm with his corroding carcinoma, a diseased breast, a kidney taken from a man gassed on the Western Front, all call forth the same plain tenderness.

At certain shelves, as I say, you have to bend and look closely, without knowing what you might see. It will be pale and strange, and possibly quite beautiful. It will be someone's catastrophe and death. Here is a femur bone with, attached, a cyst the size of a wasps' nest. Here, a rotten plum, like those we pull from our trees every year, but this someone's finger. On a low shelf are a row of balloons, shellac-coloured, they are hydrocephalic skulls. In this bending and looking, I'm reminded of Goya's *Disasters of War*, which he drew so small that to see them you must approach very close. The tiny captions Goya had appended to his images come to mind. "One cannot look at this." "This is the truth." "This is what you were born for."

~~~~~~

There are certain names we know. We know the names of the two men whose collections of anatomical specimens formed the basis of this museum. Dr John Barclay was an Edinburgh anatomist who taught classes near here and in 1821 donated his collection of comparative anatomy to the Royal College of Surgeons. Also, Sir Charles Bell, whose collection of pathological anatomy was bought in London in 1825, shipped north, and then conveyed on a gun carriage from Leith to Surgeons' Hall. Other more recent doctors added to the collection. We know these names, and also the name of the architect commissioned to design Surgeons' Hall, and sequestered within it the hall where these anatomical collections were to be housed. That architect was William Playfair, who was responsible for much of Edinburgh's Neoclassical grandeur. Consequently, this hall is known as the Playfair Hall and, like the specimens it contains, it too is fixed. Its proportions cleave to the unchanging truths of mathematics. We know the names and deeds of those men, and the many other long-dead men whose faces are fixed in oils, whose portraits hang in the corridors and function rooms of Surgeons' Hall. The names, though, of the tribe of dead whose body parts are contained here in glass jars, we do not know.

There is little we can tell of men like Barclay or Bell from their collections, no judgment we can make about these men merely by gazing at the objects they gathered around themselves. Dr Barclay was a man who could take up a tiny scalpel and flay, most delicately, the corpse of a small child until nothing remained but arteries and veins running to and from their destinations. The result hangs here in a glass closet. Around a small skeleton the blood vessels swarm stiffly, and the skeleton is arranged with arms uplifted, as though at play. For a while, in this room of still and suspended things, we must suspend judgement.

William Playfair, however, brought intelligence and compassion to his task. His room is still and elegant, a place of proportions which are, as we say, "timeless." He enclosed within the showy Royal College this place of symmetry and pallid light, wherein one moves slowly and thinks clearly. By its white elegance and its host of the passive dead, I'm reminded of the visions of heaven that used to disturb me as a child.

There are shelves, and there are also display cases, which stand on tapering legs in a line in the hall's wide aisle. In one there is a container the size of a match-box. It's made of green fish skin and holds fleams—tiny blades designed for opening veins. There are porcelain bowls decorated with flowers, into which patients would have been bled. The display cases show their contents under glass, and in so doing illustrate a distinction which William Playfair must have considered well: between being shown as an exhibit, and being housed as a specimen. The specimens, the human remains, are not exhibited in fancy cabinets. They are given the plain white shelves.

No Frankenstein extravagance, then, and other than a faint pleasant oil, half-recognised from my husband's wood work-shop, there is no smell, certainly no school-lab formaldehyde. Perhaps it is the smell of polish for the display cases or spotless floor. Aside from my own slow steps, my own occasional long-drawn breath, there is scarce any sound in the hall either.

Later in the afternoon there will be sound, because an exam is to be held in the function room next door. That room is a grand one. Light falls through a cupula, there are plaster flour-ishes decorating the walls, elaborate architraves surround the tall windows, and its walls are hung with portraits of men in piled-up curly wigs. Today the room is laid out with desks and chairs. However, so many people wish to further their careers in surgery that the doors which usually close off the Playfair Hall from the grand room of portraits, and so retain the hall's sanctity, are today hooked open, and an extra four or five desks have been prepared within the Playfair Hall itself. One candi-date, though he or she doesn't know it yet, is destined to take the farthermost desk. Therefore he or she will be sitting beside a glass case, and will have, aligned at knee height, nine skele-tons of foetuses. The first is a limp, fairy thing, almost translu-cent, but steadily they grow. Each has been arranged to stand upright as if to attention, as no foetus ever did, their bones are black and their empty eye sockets are huge within their skulls. One, the four-month-old's, stands with hands crossed in front of its groin. The finger bones are as fine as dressmakers' pins. I wonder about the candidate who must sit here, marking the paper. The answer sheets are already laid out and waiting. There will be many questions to consider, but only two possible an-swers: True or False.

"We are the geese," wrote Dr Barclay, who, after the reapers and gleaners have done their work, "still contrive to pick up a few grains . . . and waddle home in the evening, poor things, cackling with joy because of their success." By the reapers with their scythes he meant the early anatomists of modern Europe, the explorers and discoverers who, absorbed in their task, had delved ever deeper into animal or human tissue, feeling their way, peeling and following a thread of artery or sinew, making connections in their minds even as they severed them with their scalpels. With his students Barclay was popular and respected; they favoured his classes over the dreary ones offered at the university. A precise man, he lamented the slack language of anatomy. Several times, in his writings, he approached anatomy through metaphor, striving for exactitude. "The opened body is as a foreign country," he wrote, "Anatomy is as a harvest field"; "Anatomy is as to medicine as sight is to the body."

I wonder what he felt toward the objects that made up his collection. He donated them on condition that they be devoted to the purposes of "professional utility," but was there a familial affection, too? To acquire bodies, anatomists had to deal, turn blind eyes, fail to ask questions. Barclay bought some of his specimens, some were gifted, and some he dissected by his own hand. Where, I wonder, does one acquire the corpse of a toddler?

I wonder also, as I pass the jars on the shelves, here a tiny hand, there a bedraggled larynx, if the early anatomists regarded their collections with the same pride as do the collectors of stamps or tin toys. The portraits lining the corridors of the Royal College show faces which are, for the most part, concerned, intelligent and vain. Indeed, there is a marble bust of Barclay himself, which his students commissioned after his death as a mark of their esteem. You might imagine someone cadaverous, but he looks rather like an earnest dog: his head is cocked, his heavy eyebrows puckered, and his lips are parted as though he had just been asked a question and is clarifying the answer in his own mind before he replies. There are many faces, almost all men's, in the college — marble busts, and portraits hung high on the walls, but should you want to study a real nineteenth-century face, you may — that of a person whose head is preserved in a small tank. His eyes are placid and half closed in the manner of certain Buddhas, the skin is puffy and pale. To examine this face, we must kneel.

There are disasters of war in the Playfair Hall, too. In each of the window piers hangs a painting. They are by the same Charles Bell whose collection, with Barclay's, stands on the shelves around them. In 1808, Bell responded to an appeal for doctors and surgeons and hastened to Portsmouth, where thousands of soldiers, sick and hacked and shot, were being disembarked from Spain. In the face of Napoleon's attacks, the troops had been evacuated from La Coruña, and had then endured the sea voyage home. Bell treated them, and later made this series of paintings from his notes and sketches. What they show, in a sombre palette, are young men with gunshot wounds. The men are wounded in the head, the testicle, the thigh, and they display their wounds for us sorrowfully.

The first painting shows a boy shot in the upper arm. He wears a soft cap on his thick, dark hair. But for this cap, he is naked to the waist. With head lowered, and shoulder turned toward us, he gazes down at the arm he is soon to lose. The artist and doctor are one, the model and patient are one. So the young man displays his wound. The doctor has made notes. The hole in the boy's upper arm is "apparently trifling," but "when I feel thus the finger passing through the bone, this is a case for amputation." Amputation tools are displayed in the polished cabinets. There are shining saws and metal retractors. For some aesthetic or religious reason of his own, Bell has depicted the young man as though alone in a cave, like St John in the wilderness. Beyond the wounded boy, through the cave mouth, is a landscape dark with hills.

The motto of the Royal College of Surgeons is "from here, health." The surgeons have a strange motif, a hand with an eye in the palm — the "seeing hand," so called. It features on their coat of arms, which is rendered as a stained-glass window at the turn of the stair that the candidates will shortly ascend to sit their exam. The stained-glass window has this seeing hand as a centre-piece. Surrounding it are barbers' open blades, though it's hundreds of years since the Edinburgh barbers finally parted company from surgeons and formed their own guild. The seeing hand — a severed hand — faces us, the eye regards us, and below at its fingertips is a man on an operating table. He is likewise turned to face the viewer, and he hovers side-on an inch above the table. His expression is understandably doleful, and he is naked. But he has no genitals. It's a Victorian window, and not even in a Royal College of Surgeons, a place of pathologists and anatomists, could a man be shown intact. To every age, its anxieties and taboos. A hand with an eye growing in its palm, a man with no genitals: specimens of pathological anatomy both.

———

But time does pass, even in this fixed place. The techniques of preserving change. Formaldehyde came into use in the early twentieth century. Before then there was formalin, and before that cedar or linseed oil, hence the thick liquids in the oldest jars, and hence perhaps that faint sweet smell — a slow evaporation. Brandy was used too. The old jars were sealed with bitumen or pig's bladder, and the seals themselves slowly decay. Even in the specimens themselves there is change. In a vaulted cellar beneath a nearby tenement are stored those specimens not presently in the Playfair Hall. There are about six thousand all told, cared for by a collections manager. Andrew Connell is a neat, precise man in a white coat, who often works alone in a small subterranean laboratory. Today he is in the process of removing a gangrenous foot from its original preserving oils. A black crust has formed over the surface of the oil, and the blue toes protrude. The crust is a fungal growth which has developed from a spore trapped long ago in the original fluid. Even in the sealed, oxygen-depleted atmosphere within the jar, there is change and growth.

———

In the Playfair Hall, stairs lead up to the gallery. The stairs are asymmetrical, a flight in opposing corners. On the walls of the northeastern stair are watercolour drawings of more men with grotesque war injuries, this time from Waterloo. These drawings are also by Charles Bell. The ragged stumps where arms have been blown off are rendered in pastel pinks and greys. Up in the gallery are specimens which demonstrate diseases all but banished: leprosy, tuberculosis of the spine. There are skeletons of two people who suffered rickets. Their legs are shrunken and hooked up against the body like those of a bird in flight. Leaning over the white banister, I look down at the hall below with its jars of stilled disasters and diseases, its fixedness.

But nothing is truly fixed. The world changes, attitudes and taboos change. The objects in their jars have been so long dead they have outlived their function. No longer will they be carried into lecture halls and displayed to ranks of rowdy young men to illustrate a point, to describe a medical condition. Leaning over the banister, in the silent hall, I wonder what they are becoming, even as they stay the same.

<hr />

Many of the specimens are beautiful. One of the earliest is what looks like bracket fungus, but it is actually a fine slice of kidney into which the then preservator has introduced mercury. Silver threads of mercury fan through the tissue, illustrating its blood vessels. It is quite lovely; one could wear it as a brooch. You think "bracket fungus," and the tiny veins around an ectopic kidney are identical to dried lichen. There are bezoars — hard masses of indigestible material like hair or straw, which people have swallowed, and which over time have mixed with mucus and moulded to the shape of the stomach, so when removed they resemble peaches or bird's nests.

We consider the natural world as "out there," an "environment," but these objects in their jars show us the forms concealed inside, the intimate unknown, and perhaps that is their new function. Part art gallery, part church for secular contemplatives.

"In the midst of this city, you think you are removed from nature," they say — "but look within."

─────

A whole Neolithic burial, a row of tiny hands, and now I'm looking at conjoined twins. The jars are too small, they are almost squashed. There are just too many limbs. One pair has hair, and is joined at the chest. Each has but one arm — they cross as though they are hugging each other — and their mouths are close together; "but never, never canst thou kiss." I think I'm inured by now, but at the twins, finally, I want it all to stop. Here at last I want to stop gazing and just open the jar and take the twins out, to blow life into them, tell them it's okay, we can do something now. In another jar beside these twins is . . . what shall we say, what is the word? A lump, a blob: these are not good words, because it is a human thing. A fleshy lump, the size of a bag of flour. I can discern more than one mouth, some eyes, a tendril of umbilicus. The conjoined twins make me weep and I turn away, and behind is a wren, so bright, charming and complete it could have been real.

A wren, and a branch full of linnets, and the warbler which bears his name — facing the twins in their jars are the bird paintings of William MacGillivray, the naturalist who was conservator of this museum in the 1830s. His pictures of the birds he shot, then painted so exquisitely in their natural colours, enable us to see the birds clearly; they are fixed in the moment before they fly. By these pictures, we know the birds. By the specimens, we know our bodies, our conditions. In this place of silence and slow time, it's as though the conjoined twins hug each other and look happily forever upon the bright linnets and wrens. Which, I remind myself through tears, is ridiculous. But in the bodily business of weeping, I'm reminded that I'm hungry, and suddenly time begins again, and the Playfair Hall looses its sense of stilled catastrophe, and it is proper to leave.

─────

The present curator, Dawn Kemp, is an aware and intelligent woman. Later when I asked if she favoured opening the hall fully to the public, she said yes. And if there was anything she would withhold from public view? Yes — and she would accept that "elitism" might be a possible interpretation. But every age has its anxieties, its taboos and what she would withhold would be some of the foetal abnormalities. And what nowadays, if we were minded to retain body parts as messages to the future, would be considered of interest? "Interventions." The artificial valves, shunts, metal pins we carry secreted within our living flesh, often with no visible means of entry. Soon, there will be interventions at genetic level, too.

~~~

Dawn has kindly agreed to join me for lunch. We'll go down onto the street and join the warm throng of the living. We'll go to a café full of students, girls mostly. The waitress will have her bellybutton bared, someone will light a cigarette and suck the smoke down into her lungs. I want to ask Dawn many things. What she thinks these objects are, which are in her care; about the motives and morals of collectors like Dr Barclay, or Sir Charles Bell, and the unhappy provenance of the bodies they dissected, those anatomists, those "cackling geese." But before we leave her office, with its computers and books and little painted scenes of dissections and country life, Dawn shows me two more things. One she had just discovered in the back of a cupboard. She says, "You never know what you're going to find in this place, you just never know . . ." and holds out for my inspection a little blue jewellery box. It contains not a body part, but two fancy silver shoe buckles.

"James Simpson's."

James Simpson's shoe buckles! The birth of my first child was difficult; in times past it may well have killed us both. It called eventually for the interventions of ever more senior midwives, then an anaesthetist and two obstetricians. And here were Dr Simpson's shoe buckles. Had I been alone, I might have kissed them.

And a book — an Edinburgh book I'd known about for years, but had dismissed as a mawkish piece of Victoriana. Dawn, however, made me read again because *Rab and His Friends* contains a rare early description of a surgical operation. It was published in 1863, but set some thirty years earlier. Its author, John Brown, was an Edinburgh doctor. Rab, however, is a dog. Rab numbers Dr Brown among his friends, though he belongs to a carter called James Noble. When Mrs Ailie Noble, suffering terrible pain from breast cancer is taken into theatre, and in full view of the young medical students undergoes a mastectomy, Rab the dog is in theatre, too.

The author reminds us that there were no anaesthetics then. It was years before an American dentist began experimenting with ether, years before that great, kind, fleshy obstetrician Dr Simpson of the shoe buckles fell flat on the floor of his dining room, the chloroform bottle unstoppered on the table.

Mrs Noble lies down, exposes her breast. The students' hubbub is stilled. The tumour is removed, and Mrs Noble rises from the table, curtseys to the surgeon and his students, apologises if she has behaved ill and is led home to bed, where very shortly she dies. But, as though the author could sense the world was changing, he embeds in his little story about a dog a message to the future. He implores us to forgive the students, the young men who pounded upstairs into theatre, who jostled for a better view of the drama which was to unfold. He says "Don't think them heartless . . . they get over their professional horrors and into their proper work, and in them pity as an emotion ending in itself, or at least in tears and a long drawn breath, lessens — while pity as a motive is quickened and gains power and purpose. It is well for poor human nature that it is so."

Skylines

st November I was crossing Charlotte Square
ɔ glance up, saw a comet. Charlotte Square is
Georgian elegance, but on a November after-
rpopulated place. The only louche note was a
couriers lounging beneath the portico of West
Register House, waiting for their next job. I can't recall what I
was doing there, having no business with lawyers or insurance
companies, but from its wide pavements I happened to look up
and, between chimney stacks and cupolas, saw this beautiful
brass comet, a shining ball towing a deeply forked tail.

Maybe I don't look upward enough. I've known Edinburgh for
thirty-five years, even held temporary office jobs in Charlotte
Square, but never before noticed that comet. If said I knew
Edinburgh, I meant its chthonic parts, the wynds and stairs that
deliver you quickly where you're going. Before the comet, I'd
never wondered what the city raises upward; what its domes and
spires offer to the winds. Robert Adam designed the Charlotte
Square residences. I wonder if he decreed there should be a
furtive comet, too. So the comet got me wondering and, one
bright and windless day when the winter had passed, I took myself up Calton Hill to see what else I'd missed.

At three hundred feet, Calton Hill's a neat, inner-city hill,
both part of the town and elevated out of it. Even within a
lunch hour, you can ascend above the shops and traffic merely
by strolling up there. Every city needs such a hill, and if one

117

doesn't occur naturally you have to build one, like the Eiffel Tower or the London Eye.

An old stone stair leads from Waterloo Place up onto the hill. The sun was creeping along the walls and, half-hid by ivy and with old-fashioned understatement, a painted sign informed us that "interesting and attractive views of Edinburgh and its environs could be had" from its monuments. And it's true. When you emerge onto the grassy summit, you can behold what Patrick Geddes, the Edinburgh champion of town planning, called the "synoptic view" — a seeing of the city as a whole, and with your own eyes.

It's a dramatic place. The land which descends in a long slope from the Pentland Hills northward till it meets the shores of the Firth of Forth is interrupted by the cores of extinct volcanoes. The Calton Hill is one, the Castle Rock another, and Arthur's Seat the daddy of them all. Confined between them, as water flows between rocks, are tenements, spires, domes. A place of wind and northern sunlight, and robust architecture, the city sends one down steps and through pends, under bridges, between tenements, then, like the reward for a life of Presbyterian constraint, offers one sudden Neoclassical façades, or blue glimpses of the sea.

The cloudless February sky arched over the city, clear but for a couple of contrails which held their shape out toward the airport in the west, and the city was at my feet. At my back was the architectural assemblage, the monuments and memorials that give the hill its peculiar, sternly comic atmosphere.

There is the colossal business of the National Monument, which was intended to be a full-blown copy of the Parthenon, to honour the dead of the Napoleonic Wars, but the project ran out of steam and it remains unfinished. Its columns cast long shadows on the grass. There's a memorial to Nelson, a tower shaped somewhat like a telescope; a square Greek temple honours Playfair the architect; a little round one is dedicated to a philosopher called Dugald Stewart. But despite all the dead the Calton Hill is a lively place — it's a well-known gay cruising area, a vista for tourists, a lunchtime break for workers in the offices, and it has shops at its feet.

I walked around, then chose a spot under the boundary wall of the hill's oldest building, the Observatory. Gothic tower meets Pictish hillfort — Robert Adam had a hand in this, too — it was built in 1790, when the sky over Edinburgh was still dark at night, and the population confined to the long slope that runs the mile from the Castle Rock to Holyrood. On that ridge the tenements grew like mushrooms on a log, until it became, in Patrick Geddes's words, "the most overcrowded and deteriorated of all the world's cities." From my place facing west, I had the Old Town, picturesque and hugger-mugger on one hand; on the other, the ordered and rectangular plan of the New, and beyond on all sides the reach and sound of the modern city.

The February sun was so warm I hooked my coat on a railing and began to assemble the telescope. Below, the city's spires and roofs looked at once robust and vulnerable, like an organism which is both living and stone, coral perhaps, more brittle than you'd imagine when you're tramping its streets. As well as chimneys and steeples, what the streets yielded up was a constant traffic noise, pierced now and then by a clang of metal or a builder's yell — they are gutting the old GPO building nearby, there are cranes and scaffolding. Most loud in my own ear, though, was the fruity little song of a robin. The sky was unbroken blue, shading to a dusty pink over the hills and the islands of the Firth lay as though at anchor. On the far side of the Firth, the coast of Fife, a train slipped from one small town to the next.

There is something slightly hallucinogenic about looking through a telescope, something Peter-Pannish about being able to swoop over rooftops. It feels — and looks — illicit. Greedy, too. With my eye to the lens, I had the city in my lap and could hoard to myself an unfair share of steeples and spires and cupolas; crow-stepped gables, garrets and all the Old Town's lums came rushing toward me. Some of the spires are well-known, like the Gothic rocket of the Scott Monument, and the castle, of course, high on its rock. With a tweak of the focus knob, though, I could conjure up little parties of tourists leaning over its battlements. A few degrees left, and the hugger-mugger of the Old Town resolved itself into an open garret window here, with orange curtains, or there, a ladder leaning precipitously from a roof up onto a disorderly row of chimneypots.

Prompted by the comet, I wanted to see the finishing touches, the glints of brass or lead or gold. Wondering quite where to begin, I trained the telescope toward Charlotte Square, but the comet was too fugitive, not raised high enough above roofs to be seen. What marked Charlotte Square was the green dome of West Register House. I tweaked the focus dial, and saw for the first time the sullen cross it raises toward the sky. But I resolved to be systematic, to look at things in turn, rather than as a magpie, lighting on shiny objects at random.

Perhaps it's a function of Edinburgh's Protestantism, but few people were raised on high. No saints, and precious few heroes. Only Henry Dundas, the Viscount Melville, who stands on a tall column in the gardens of St Andrews Square. A man of such power, they called him "the uncrowned kind of Scotland." Round his neck is a lightning conductor, uncomfortably like a noose. There is a woman, though, who sails aloft on the dome of the Bank of Scotland HQ. The bank stands at the top of the Mound, bearing down upon the prosperous New Town as though to remind it of exactly who's boss. In Scotland's capital city Fame faces firmly south. Green with verdigris — not an unbecoming shade — and draped in robes, she holds in her hands two laurel wreaths. She is about to cast them away, to bestow them onto some unsuspecting pedestrian far below. For all the grandiose Baroque nonsense beneath her bare feet, Fame stands as stylish and bored as a cruise passenger playing quoits.

Warming to the task now, I nudge the telescope a little east. Fame wears some sort of Greek drapery, but there is a gilded Youth so startlingly naked you wonder how they got away with it — probably because he's a denizen of the rooftops, and the douce folk of Edinburgh weren't then equipped with telescopes. A Youth, with the sun falling full upon him, he at least is a weel-kent Edinburgh figure, he strands mid-stride on the dome on top of the university's Old College. His task is to carry aloft the flaming Torch of Knowledge, which he does with athletic ease. They say Edinburgh is a dualistic place, though, and you could well imagine the Youth climbing down, to stride gleaming across the South Bridge toward Calton Hill, looking for a different sort of knowledge, like that poem of Cavafy's when a god comes down to the city, "tall, extremely handsome, the joy of being immortal in his eyes." I was almost embarrassed to be seen inspecting him, but the youth has to be big, to be in keeping with the building he completes. I know that building from university days. Beneath the Youth is a dome and, beneath the dome, an awesome block of Neoclassicism which makes the passing double-deckers look dainty. There's thundering Latin inscription about kings and MDCCLXXXIX, and ARCHITECTO ROBERTO ADAM — lest we forget — and below that is a triumphal arch, and through the arch the youthful students pass, draped in baggy denims, bearing mobile phones.

Old College was Robert Adam's swan-song, if that's the word, because he died before it was done, and the project was taken over by others, and it ran out of money, and a century went by before the dome and its famous Youth were completed. The Youth faces east, so he will never know Fame. She is always at his back, but he can glance down, if he deigns, at Holyrood, where, little more than half a mile away, its architect dead, fabulously over-budget, the new Scottish Parliament has recently been revealed.

I panned west just a little, and caught the crescent moon on the minaret of the new Southside mosque, then scanned the flat roofs of the modern university blocks, which offer not fancy finials, but twentieth-century aerials and telecommunication masts. Then, a swivel of the lever, a turn of the dial and, so close in my sights I could have shot it, was the cockerel that crows from St Giles. St Giles Cathedral rises clear above the Old Town roofs, its spire is a crown-shape and unmistakable. Nothing unusual there — a cockerel on a church weather vane is more common in cities than the real thing. It was gold-coloured, splendid in the morning light, but in close-up was a queer-like bird. He had the required arched and plumed tail, but being raised on a pole made him leggy, and his beak was so long that, frankly, it looked like a redshank's. An odd beast, but it could have been swivelling up there for five hundred years, so it was entitled to look peculiar. The word "cathedral" has stuck from pre-Reformation days, they say it's a wonder the building itself wasn't torn down, so the cockerel's survived well, swinging with the various winds.

Then, again among the welter of Old Town garrets and gables, was a wrought-iron weather vane. This was what we wanted, the secret, modest things half-hid among the roofs, like animals in a forest. This device was oddly nautical, the arrow was a trident and the board, which the wind clapped, shaped a bit like a ship's wheel. It had been wind-battered once too often, though, and listed to starboard. What building it belonged to I couldn't tell; doubtless one I'd passed a thousand times, perhaps even entered. Neither could I tell which nearby steeple lifted toward the skies a strange, rust-coloured, eight-pointed star. Eight points, not six, gave it a busy, overexcited look. A star, a ship's wheel, a daft medieval cockerel — we were doing well.

⁓

It was mid-morning and people were up strolling on the hill. They passed behind me, singly or in groups, tourists mostly. I heard Spanish and American voices, and felt a bit self-conscious, like a Peeping Tom, but the only window I looked into was the Queen's, who wasn't in town. I can tell you that she keeps a devilish bright-red lion hunkered among the battlements of Holyrood Palace. One passer-by, a Japanese girl, asked if I would take her photo with the whole of Edinburgh as a backdrop. Another, an Irishman, asked if I was birdwatching, so we spoke about city birds, and the sparrow hawks he saw regularly, and the buzzard he spotted at the top of Leith Walk. He went on his way and I resolved to look for sparrow hawks, too, up among the weathercocks. The only birds visible were herring gulls resting on chimneypots, or cruising over the rooftops like pieces flaked off from the city's skin.

The castle, being rugged and defensive, offered little to the wind but its own ramparts and battlements and, tucked amongst them, a few grudging golden balls. Near at hand, though, was the clock-tower of the Balmoral hotel. It was so close the clock face filled the telescope's sights, and it was weird because, like the White Rabbit's watch, the minute hand moves constantly—as if always running to keep up, to cover a minute's distance in a mere sixty seconds. To see it magnified was to suffer a moment's panic, a horrible sensation that life and time is running away.

By custom, this clock is set fast, because it rises above the station and everyone consults it who has a train to catch. Everyone looks at the clock, but who sees above it, at the very top of its square tower, a secret little room. Trapped within a wrought-iron affair like a birdcage, is a tiny room. I could even see inside: wood-panelled, painted white, with just space enough for a table and chair. Of all the rooms in that grand hotel, this is surely the best. Perhaps they could keep a philosopher there, like one of those picturesque hermits great lords kept in their policies. A philosopher to tell us about time and identity; how this hotel was for long the *North British*, but now it's the *Balmoral*, even as it stays the same; how the site where it stands was once a marsh, the station once a physic garden; how city ever rises into being, even as it falls away. Above the caged room, a saltire hung limp about its pole.

It strains the eyes, all this looking and refocusing. I had counted five cockerels, some flighted arrows, a star, a trident, a golden youth, a lady playing hoopla, a preposterous globe held up by fat babies, a moon, an astrolabe (this on the new Standard Life building), a red lion. Shrink them, and you could wear them as a charm bracelet, the city round your wrist. And, of course, there were crosses, some as intricate as snowflakes, the pinnacles of churches which once were great, but which are slowly forgetting their purpose. Nightclubs and bars inhabit them now, the way hermit crabs inhabit the shells of whelks.

I'd developed an instant affection for the city's cockerels and went looking for more. About a mile away southwest rose two close together. Farmyard rivals, you might say. One surmounted a pennant worked with the letters "R.I." If "R.I." was the Royal Infirmary, the other had to be announcing George Heriot's School. Two hundred years and two hundred yards separate the two birds; Heriot's from within its private gardens and, across the street, the hospital. It grieves me to say it, for it's a private school for the wealthy, but Heriot's is cock o' the walk, the best-dressed chicken in town. It shines, it crows, it's the best detailed, its tail is the most plumed, its legs are two legs, not a mere pole. The school's founder was goldsmith to the king, so perhaps he gave particular mind to these matters.

Heriot's School is a square, with towers at each corner. The Infirmary is so very Victorian, Florence Nightingale herself approved its design. Its weathercock stands high on a cone-shaped tower, a pinnacle pierced with windows and louvred ventilators. You can't see it from here, of course, but above the Infirmary door is another bird, carved in stone. Not a cockerel, but a pelican feeding its young with the blood of its own breast. On either side, the words "I was a stranger and ye took me in, I was sick and ye visited me." They are majestic words, but now gossipy banners hang from the hospital's turreted windows. "Did you know? The Royal Infirmary is now closed." The hospital is closed, the sick trundled furth of the city to some place beyond sight, beyond walking distance, and the hospital site given over to developers. Nightingales, pelicans and cockerels notwithstanding, its gates are padlocked closed.

It's obvious, but perhaps worth repeating, that everything raised is raised deliberately, nothing falls upward by accident. Everything the city lifts above itself has been given thought and design. Thought and design, then allotted a secretive existence, glimpsed now and again by the streetbound. Having never properly looked up as I made my way to shops and work and lectures, or sat exams, visited the sick, drank in pubs, endured Fringe shows in freezing churches, checked the time as I ran for trains, I'd never before realised that what we catch sight of on the city roofs are symbols.

An eight-pointed star, for example, is a symbol of regeneration — but who knows that? I had to look it up. The church that wears it is the Tron, which hasn't been used as a church for a long time. It stands on the corner of the High Street and South Bridge and was for an age the town's Hogmanay gathering place. I knew its robust spire because friends have a third-floor flat directly opposite, and the Tron's big shiny clock face looms into their sitting room. From their windows you can easily read the inscription, which tells of a great fire. The original steeple burned down, there were streams of molten lead. This new steeple was erected in 1820. All this I know, but I'd never before noticed its star.

The city sends up noise and fumes, and also the symbols of the day, the zeitgeist cast in shining brass and lifted skyward. But symbols, with their exact, non-negotiable "meaning" fall out of use, even as they remain above our heads. From the hill here you can focus in on hundreds of years' worth cluttering the skyline. When we can no longer read them, we have to look up in books. They become curiosities. "Did you know," we might say, "that the cockerel is an emblem of St Peter? A ninth-century Papal edict required every church to raise one." "Did you know the pelican is a Christian symbol of charity?" Developers wrangle with the town planners about the Infirmary site. They want to build flats twelve storeys high. And what will the cockerel do then, poor thing? At present, a symbol in danger of becoming a metaphor, he's a green and sickly bird.

A helicopter, following the line of the Pentland hills, passed silently behind the dark, slender spire of the Tolbooth Kirk, which is now a club. In the same moment, a moment delicately choreographed, a long jib of a crane, carrying an iron girder, swung into the telescope's sights.

What you have to look harder for are the simple, arrow-shaped wind vanes which carry no weight of meaning, but are mere messengers of change. To find wind vanes, and the devices they're mounted upon which name the four compass points, you have to poke about among the chimneys and aerials of the skyline, because they tend to belong to buildings which are less high and less grand. There was that jaunty, nautical one with the ship's wheel, but to my mind the most stylish is the arrow on St Cuthbert's at the east end of Princes Street Gardens. Over the gardens, I had clear line of sight, although the church is well below street level. And although the trains pass nearby, blaring their horns before they enter a tunnel, there is birdsong down there and trees, and entire Victorian families lie buried in its walled grounds. Helplessly dominated by the castle rock, the steeple nonetheless braves on up, to hold above its quiet graveyard a stylised flighted arrow, pewter grey.

Framed in the telescope's sights, the arrow held quite still. All the city's weathervanes and banners and weathercocks held still. All the clocks were in rough agreement; it was getting on for lunchtime, and people were climbing the hill to sit in the sun and eat their sandwiches. I began to fold up the telescope, resolved to come back on a blustery day, to catch that dynamic moment when, unnoticed by its citizens, the wind veers, and above the traffic and business all the city weather vanes swivel at once.

So I offer this observation, which won't stand scrutiny. In the olden days, when every city was a garden city, before every scrap of land was built on and cities became slums, what was raised up high were cockerels. Then, in Robert Adam's time, the Enlightenment, came the Youth Bearing Knowledge. On the Victorians' slender spires are crosses which look delicate, but which must actually be thumping great weights of metal. In the late twentieth century, when roofs became flat, we dispensed with God and raised aerials and antennae, the apparatus of communications with one another. There are more domestic, whimsical things, too: a comet, a cat, a raven. But the winds have changed again. The city's newest building is immediately below the Calton Hill; you can look directly down on it. A twenty-first-century affair, of smoked glass, presence and inclusion, cinemas and escalators and bars, the Omni building promises leisure for all. What it raises on its roof is a garden. You can't see it from the street, of course — you have to climb the hill.

Sabbath

On the headland, as though looking out to sea, were many cairns built of stones. They came into view as you walked up through the wicket gate toward the clifftop, and you'd think them the recent work of tourists with time on their hands, but when you got close you could see they were whiskery with green lichen. You might fancy them the petrified remains of people who'd spent too long sitting in contemplation. Or built by people who'd known they had to head back to their lives, but wanted something of themselves to remain here, forever gazing at the sea. The headland was covered with them, some shaped like old-fashioned beehives, others like houses of cards, with uprights and horizontals. With these ones, you could bend and look at the sea as though through a letterbox.

I found a place well back from the cliff edge, out of the wind, and sat down. To the south a cliffy headland jutted out into the sea, and round its end gannets kept coming in threes or fours, heading north, all but invisible until they tilted into the sunlight and then their white wings gleamed. The horizon was interrupted only by the Flannan Isles, where according to the ballad the light-house keepers had so simply, so mysteriously, disappeared.

It was still early. I sat on a damp rock, took my notebook from my inner pocket, made earnest notes:

"South — sky thin line of rosy pink, straightened blue-pink, blue-greys. Flannan Isles, horizon fine slate-grey line. [unreadable] 3 gannets."

I made notes, but the reason I'd come to the end of the road to walk along the cliffs is because language fails me there. If we work always in words, sometimes we need to recuperate in a place where language doesn't join up, where we're thrown back on a few elementary nouns. Sea. Bird. Sky.

Besides, it was the Sabbath, the day of rest. A sign at the wicket gate that gave onto the coastal walk read: "Please, keep dogs on leads," and "Please, avoid disturbing the Sabbath."

It was summer's end — I had a few days to clear my head. The summer had been hard going, with one greater or minor family crisis after another. There was our grandmother, whom we call Nana, slipping into dependency, and my mother who was adjusting to life at home having been paralysed by a major stroke, and my scared heroic dad doing his best; there were the needs of our small children to be met, and then my daughter had missed her first ever day at school because she was in hospital having a head wound closed. But the summer had passed, and already, like migrant birds, my university students were arriving, waiting for the teaching term to begin, expecting to be taught how to engage with the world in langauge.

Keeping the sea to my left hand I walked northwards, the way the gannets had indicated. The clifftop land dipped into damp troughs and then rose onto promontories where bedrock broke through the thin earth. There were pools of peaty water between rocks, and foraging parties of golden plover. You might call it a wild place, what with the Atlantic to one hand and peat bog to the other, but in each saddle between the headlands was evidence of some human intervention, an enclosure or a wall. In one I saw the undulations of old lazy beds. Cruel misnomer: looking down from above, they resembled beds right enough, like sleepers blanketed in peat, but they spoke of hard graft, of carting creels of kelp from the shore to fertilise the thin soil, to extract a hard living from the land.

I walked up onto the next headland, and there in the next

bay was a sea-stack, a hundred foot or so high. It didn't stand out proud, commanding the ocean, but shrank almost shyly at the back of a dark forbidding concavity of cliff. I dared forward to look down at the water and could see it wasn't a true stack, not truly free-standing but joined to the cliff behind it by an untidy rocky causeway. Nonetheless, the fulmars loved it. They rested in its ledges, or tipped off the rough pinnacle to glide effortlessly about.

There seemed to be something on its summit. Not a person, surely, but perhaps another of those odd cairns. I lifted the binoculars, turned the focus wheel with my thumb until I had in view an impossible little building, no more than a cell. There was a doorway of sorts, but the lintel had long slewed sideways, the whole edifice was leaning at a crazy angle. Whatever it was, hermitage or lookout post, it had the aura of something very old, possibly prehistoric, and it was falling into the sea. A saint or sentry creeping out of that tiny doorway, eyes full of light and ears full of surf, would have to be careful; one false step and he'd pitch clean over the edge and plummet down through the indifferent fulmars into the water below.

But there was something appealing about it. To live alone in a stone cell on a sea-stack, the fulmars for neighbours, the Atlantic breakers and the crying wind; so what if it was slewing to one side? To reach it, you would have to climb. You'd need ropes and harnesses, and you'd have to carry your provisions in a creel on your back. With the glasses, I tried to pick out a route. Perhaps as second, following a trusted leader on a very tight rope, I could try to feel my way up. It would smell of guano and mineral, and at that moment I could almost remember, from my youth, the intimate feel of rock.

Twenty years ago I had a boyfriend called Peter who was a rock climber thrilled with the stretch and fluidity of the body. He's a senior physiotherapist now, charged with restoring broken bodies to function, if not to grace. I called him when my mother was in rehab learning to walk again after her stroke, for an honest opinion of her prospects, and I thought about him again now as I looked through the glasses at this stack. I recall him shouting down at me once, when I was struck with fear half-way up some rockface: "Remember! It's your skeleton that holds the position, not the muscles. You can let the muscles relax."

"I can't do this!" I'd wailed.

"You are doing it," he'd replied.

I put the binoculars away to move on. I'd find out what it was, this strange inaccessible cell. The mood I was in, it would suit me just fine. I'd look it up in Stornoway Library. I'd look it up in one of the estate agents' windows.

—————

The week before I'd come to Lewis, I'd spent a day with my sister in our parents' home town in the west. We'd come to see our grandmother. Every other weekend, someone drives over to see our grandmother. She is either in her own tiny flat, with its gas fire and armchair and plaster dolphins leaping on the mantelpiece, or, as today, in the ward of the hospital she's frequently admitted to. There had been a phone call; someone telling me they were even now breaking the door down, lifting Nana from the floor where she'd lain all night, carrying her to the ambulance, taking her again into hospital.

None of the family lives in that town these days. Our parents left when they were young and first married, and now that our mother is herself suddenly disabled and our father charged with her care, and we children already approaching middle age with infants and bread-winning responsibilities of our own, Nana's situation is a constant anxiety.

We had come together, my sister and me, with appointments to see social workers and doctors. In windowless offices we'd signed long forms and discussed doctors' opinions and money. Nana had been a cleaner much of her life, and a single parent: not wealthy. We'd been given a list of care homes for the elderly in that town, and then we went to have a difficult conversation with Nana herself.

She was sitting in a green high-backed chair in a hospital day room, one old lady among the rest, dressed like the others in a blouse and cardigan and loose trousers. With great attention to detail, she told us what had been served for lunch. We, her two granddaughters, sat before her. My sister held her hand and at last we put the case that had been building over the preceding few years.

Around us were other old women, and old men sitting on chairs identical to our nana's. There were tables with magazines, a TV which was always switched on. Sunlight glinted off the cars parked outside. Now and then snatches of other conversations reached us, cheery banter pitched loud enough for the hard of hearing. I longed to be back outdoors. As we entered my sister had said, "When she sees us both together, she'll think something's wrong. She'll think Mum's had another stroke or something," and I, never skilled at small talk, thought of news to tell her, tried to dredge up incidents from family life. I rehearsed the story of my daughter's gashed head, and the stitches.

We were surrounded by the very old. The woman in the next chair was asleep, her chin reaching her chest. Next along was a woman who was awake. She wore a blue knitted cardigan — or rather, because her shoulders and breasts sloped at odd, tilting angles, a blue cardigan had been arranged round her. Though we were talking to our own grandmother, too loudly for such a delicate conversation, I could see out of the corner of my eye a tiny persistent movement, as you might see a spider in a corner of a window. A little table was pulled up in front of the woman in blue, and on it stood a carton of orange juice. The old woman was struggling to get the end of the straw into the tiny foil-covered hole. The bony hand, the feeble, stabbing straw, the carton, which at any moment would go skiting off the table onto the floor, all became intolerable, so I went and asked if I could help. "Thank you, my dear," she said. "Thank you."

The gannets had come to Dalmore, which is a surfers' bay, but no surfers were out this Lord's day. White waves surged in between twin headlands, and the gannets, not feeding, not breeding, not going any place, were turning and lifting on the winds. Among the dunes at the top of Dalmore Bay is the cemetery. It is enclosed in stone walls and defences had been built to prevent the sea from disturbing the graves. Of course, you'd be more likely to approach the cemetery from the landward side: there is a thin island road that ends at its gate. The headstones stand in neat rows; plots yet to be occupied were marked with numbered metal labels. Presumably there are people who have wandered from this parish all over the world, but who know their number, who carry in their heads an image of this burial ground at the end of the thin road, at the bay.

From the cemetery, I followed the road inland. The township's houses were shut up for the Sabbath. Even the dogs were quiet; one watched me pass from a doorstep, his head on its paws, only his brown eyes moving. Only one house betrayed life, and that by condensation on its windows. I walked self-consciously, noting wire fences, disused cars, peat stacks, wondering if to be moving at all, making a display of oneself through the stillness of the afternoon, was to disturb the Sabbath. Sheep were bleating, though. Penned in the infields, ewes with fat lambs bleated and bleated. Perhaps they knew it would soon be time for the lambs to be taken away.

A friend said to me — we were talking about our stage in life, when we suddenly discover that we are the grown-ups, with children and parents, and even grandparents to tend to, not to mention our pupils, patients or clients or employers — that we spend so much time dealing with it all, there is scarcely time to feel. I walked up the silent road, wondering if I couldn't reconcile myself again to the idea of the Sabbath, to the day of dreary silence and mutton broth I'd known as a child, if we couldn't close the shops and still the traffic and institute a modern, churchless day of contemplation and rest; and if it would help at all.

The little hostel was surprisingly busy. It's one of a cluster of half a dozen blackhouses some distance above a rocky shore. They're pretend blackhouses, reconstructed for tourists, with curved thatched roofs, thick stone walls and tiny windows. A pretend blackhouse, because there is no peat fire in the middle of the floor. There are Calor Gas stoves, and electricity.

There were people round the table from Spain and Germany, Australia and England. There were youngsters who'd just finished college and were about to look for their first job, and, almost old enough to be their parents, the jaded and weary, like myself and the Australian chemistry teacher who'd taken a year's leave and been living out of a car for months.

"Quite right, too," I said. "Do it while you can. *Carpe Diem* and all that."

"Are you Scottish?" she said. We were sitting at the black-house gable in the last of the light.

"Not from here. From the other side of the country."

"Holiday?"

"Few days to clear my head before the term starts."

"You are so lucky. I had to come right round the world for this."

There was a young man called Tom, who had straggly blond hair and a bike with a trailer. He must have been superbly fit, because after I'd made his acquaintance I saw him everywhere, for the next few days, from Mealista to Stornoway, beating along the single-track roads, grinning, in love with the world.

"What did you do today?" I asked him. He was repairing a tyre.

"Went to church! I don't, usually. Just wanted to know what it was about, you know?"

"And what was it about?"

"I don't know. It was in Gaelic. A twenty-minute sermon and I couldn't understand a word. But you should have heard the sweetie-rustling! But that psalm singing was amazing, like nothing I'd ever heard before, not even on my African tapes."

"What about yourself?" he asked. "What did you do?"

"Me?" I said. "I just wandered along the cliffs."

"Cool."

It had never entered my head, this Sunday, to go to church.

———

I'd called all the old people's homes on the list the social worker had given us, and for the next few days the postman had pushed through my letterbox leaflets and brochures, pictures of dining rooms and bedrooms, always empty. One showed an entrance hall. The carpet was tartan, the walls were papered in a different, clashing tartan. Dolls dressed in black velvet stood like sleepwalkers on one sideboard; on another was a tank of hapless tropical fish. A huge clock, like a sunburst, ticked away the minutes of the days. It looked like the antechamber to hell, but when I phoned I heard much cheerful laughter in the background. I'd to ask, "Do you have a waiting list, and how long . . . ?"

"Well," the woman had said, "when someone demits . . ."

Demit — I'd to look it up. A Scots word, it means "relinquish."

———

A few days to clear my head, I'd said, and it was true. But where to go? "To the end of the road," I told myself, and the notion pleased me. So I'd hired a car. I'd been to one road-end and walked up to the strange cairns and the cell atop the stack — but there were a couple more days and there were more island roads. I thought "Why not go to them, too?" Go to all the ends of all the roads and see what's there.

So, when the Sabbath was over and washing flapped on the lines, I followed a road over peat-moor, where the peat banks were freshly cut, and shone as brown as polished leather in the sun. I passed a blighted pine plantation and a man working at his croft with a scythe. I passed newly built, unlet business units. There were knapweed and yellow coltsfoot in the ditches, not a cloud in the sky. At times the road turned inland, across peat bog, between lochans, and at times it followed the

shore, offering sudden vistas of yellow beaches and low, distant, dark-purple promontories. There were few other vehicles
on the single-track road: mostly vans — working lads travelling
at speed. I tucked into a passing place to allow a huge, empty
livestock lorry, doubtless come for lambs, to inch by. It was a
hot day, such vast light. Tethered in sea lochs were fish farms
and mussel farms. I drove down to a jetty and left the car to listen for a minute to a stack of lobster creels that was twittering
with starlings as they picked scraps.

Inland the hills rose stony and pale and unshadowed, as in
Greece or Italy. At Uig, I pulled into a passing place to let an
approaching vehicle go by. It wasn't a lorry come for lambs,
but a black hearse. Within its stately windows the coffin shone,
brass handles gleaming in sunlight. The two undertakers lifted
their hands in acknowledgment as they went, bearing the coffin on its way. There would be a walled burial ground, perhaps
at the end of a bay, at the end of a road.

Feeling as though I had strayed into a film, I carried on, past
the houses of Islivig. Where the road ended, there was a five-
bar gate, with a sign hung on it: "Common Grazing."

I parked and wandered down to the shore. Half-buried in
the green turf were the ruins of an ancient convent. Someone
had knocked together a cross out of driftwood, and hung a sign
on it: "Tigh na cailleach dubh" — The place of the black [-veiled]
women. I walked within its walls, wondering what it would be
like to be a nun, black-veiled and in retreat from the world.
Out in the bay the sea was glassy blue, bar where waves broke
to white over a hidden reef. A lobster boat moved slowly between two islands. From the corner of my eye, though, I noticed a quick dark movement about the seaweed of the tidal
rocks. It was a mink, the interloper and arch predator, enemy
of sea birds.

Back on the track again, a young man was striding toward
me, with blood on his tweeds. Not blood, I thought, I'm becoming overwrought. It must be mud, he's a farm lad, a crofter.

"Is it always like this here?" I said of the clear skies.

"I wish," he replied.

Three other men were processing down from the hill, one dragging the carcass of a stag over the rough ground, then a man with a gun in a case, then a third man, hauling another stag. They made slow progress and looked for a moment like a framed print you might find on the wall of a country pub. There was the sudden noise of an engine and the bloodstained man brought a pick-up truck to meet the shooting party as they gained the road. Together they heaved the dead animals into the back, so only a rack of antlers stuck up over the side. Then the truck moved off along the thin road between hill and shore.

In Stornoway's big supermarket, I thought, maybe it's a language problem. Maybe the world would make more sense if you could think about it in a different language. Once, some years ago, I'd met an angry young Gael who said he was fed up with people treating his islands like a sort of Eden, who came to "escape," but who refused to learn Gaelic. I could learn Gaelic. Right here, I could learn the Gaelic for "tea" and "coffee," "cat-food" and "tinned vegetables," from the signs hung over the aisles where the people push their trolleys. Gaelic for "cornucopia." I could learn place names from the dual-language road signs and the Ordnance Survey map. One language breathing down the neck of the other. The painted sign on the five-bar gate at the road end was in English: "Common Grazing," it said. Yet the sign beside the ruins of the convent — that had read "Tigh na cailleach dubh." When, at Na Gearrannan/ Garenin, I'd passed two men in blue overalls conversing over a gate, they'd been speaking in Gaelic but gave me the time of day in English. When their collie trotted after me it was called back and apologies offered me, in English.

The librarian in Steornabhagh/ Stornoway was an Englishman, a Geordie I think. He brought me old maps and gazetteers to look at. I was hoping to find out about that wild building on the sea-stack. Someone had taken a red biro to the old maps, scored out the Anglicised names and re-substituted the Gaelic.

In the window of the newsagent's, a few doors along the

street, were two little black and white printed notices, each announcing a funeral. They were in English. The language of the service, and the graveside murmurings, I don't know. The language of the schoolchildren scaling down the hill from the Nicolson Institute, girls in black skirts, a boy calling to his mates as he skateboarded along — that was English. The people standing outside the newsagent's, waiting for the English papers to come in off the plane, were speaking together in Gaelic. I could learn Gaelic, learn every language under the sun, but I don't know if it would help.

~

Yesterday, other than a couple of civil greetings to strangers, I'd spoken to no one, which was fine by me. Today, two or three shops had notices in their windows, saying they'd be observing a minute's silence because it was September 11th, the anniversary of all those deaths. Minutes of silence, of remembrance. A momentary Sabbath. I'd watched the Twin Towers on TV as I knelt on the floor of a guesthouse in the Lake District. I'd been booked to give a poetry reading that night, at Grasmere, home of Wordsworth. Did I want to cancel, they asked? I said no. It's poetry's job, isn't it, to keep making sense of the world in language, to keep the negotiation going? We can't relinquish that. A surprising number of people came to hear the poetry, considering.

"Minute's silence!" a friend had snarled. "Did they not know, the silence-keepers, how many children had died even that morning in Angola, in Sudan, just because they had no clean water? Was there to be a minute's silence for them?" A minute's silence for each, and the world would be hushed forever.

Perhaps, though, if we join up all these minutes we are beginning secularly to observe, we could string them together in a new kind of Sabbath, where there are no men in black blighting our lives with their notions of sin, no chaining up the children's swings for the Lord's day. I mean a contemplative time, a time reserved to reflect. Perhaps we would feel less imperilled.

I called home, standing with my mobile phone on a street that smelled of peat smoke. Everything was okay. Nothing had gone wrong. My daughter said, "Hello Mummy, I can't find my homework."

"How's your head?" I asked

"Oh, it's fine."

My husband said, "Elaine called. She seemed a bit upset." So I called Elaine, who told me what had happened. Her colleague at work had turned up as usual, then after an hour made some excuse to leave. He had then driven to a certain spot in a beautiful part of the country, among mountains and lochs, the kind of place one might go to think things through in peace. There he had killed himself. As she told me about this man's solitary drive, it brought to mind the images of my own: the five-bar gate, the vaulting sky, the islands set in a turquoise sea, the mink worrying among the rocks.

Everything will fall into the sea, so far as I could tell, looking at the archaeologists' reports in Stornoway Library. Does this matter? A team of archaeologists had walked and mapped all the features on that part of the coast and, with their expert eye, and by dint of asking local people, had measured and defined and assessed every human intervention in that landscape: illicit stills, sheep fanks, standing stones. Their anxiety was coastal erosion, things were in danger of slipping away forever. The report itself had been poorly bound, pages slithered out and fell on the library floor.

There was mention of the little building on the stack. It had been labelled, and numbered. The report said the little building was prehistoric and in imminent danger of collapse, but I still don't know what it was. No one had dared climb up to it.

When I'd called Peter, the rock-climber and physiotherapist, to ask his opinion on my mother's chances, he was about to enter his forty-third year, which he was doing with some trepidation because at that age his own father had died.

"And we're trying to find a home for our grandmother," I was saying. "Och, it's awful."

"Why is it awful?"

Not for the first time, I failed to find an answer to Pete's brusque Yorkshire questions.

"Granny's at that stage in life — you're in yours. It's not awful."

"I can't do it!" I wailed, half in jest.

"You are doing it." he replied.

~~~

I'd envied Tom his bike, so hired one of my own, then went cycling out of Stornoway on a grey, unsettled morning. I cycled around traffic islands with palm shrubs, mistook a turn and pedalled past the hospital and through a council scheme before finding the coast road north. I rode under a grey sky that threatened rain, relishing the movement of my body, its own small continuing strength. It wouldn't last forever — that was the truth of it — but today I could cycle along a road, to see where it led.

There were low, rendered houses, a pharmacy, a big serious church, and then I was alone with moor to my left side; to the right, the waters of the Minch and the distant mainland mountains. When the road neared its end, it descended in a great hill to the huge beach at Tolsta. Black-backed gulls and kittiwakes formed two distinct parties at the shoreline, all facing into the wind. A drizzle had set in, and then it turned to real rain. At an empty car park beside a lily-filled lochan the metalled road became a track, which in turn became a churned-up peaty path leading onto the moor. But: there was a bridge. In the middle of the peat bog was a grand single-span Victorian bridge. I leaned the bike on the stone parapet, watched the water coursing below. The bridge — they call it the "Bridge to Nowhere" — was one of Lord Leverhulme's grand schemes. Landlord of Lewis in the 1880s, he'd thought up many a plan for the island: a railway, a kelp industry, a castle at Stornoway now boarded and disused. At the Bridge to Nowhere, I turned back.

I'd missed, of course, the minute's silence — I'd been free-wheeling downhill at the time, bawling old Rod Stewart songs aloud to myself. Instead I stopped in the tiny garden that encloses the Tolsta war memorial. The bronze plaque lists too many names for this small place; the same surnames recur over and again. The memorial, in the shape of an open book, also remembers the many soldiers who were returning to Lewis from the Great War, only to be drowned when their ship, the *Iolaire*, struck rocks outside Stornoway Harbour, which is a difficult one to make sense of. There are memorials, too, to the "heroes of the land struggle" — men who'd made it home and demanded not railways or bridges or castles, but land. "All the crofts of Upper Bac lie on land so seized."

We would soon have to arrange, my sister and I, to sell our grandmother's tiny tenement flat to pay for her care in her last years. The back kitchen would have to be relinquished, the armchair and plaster dolphins taken away.

At the end of the road there is a burial ground, enclosed in a stone wall. But we know that. There are other roads, which may end variously. There might be a five-bar gate, with a hand-painted sign opening onto common grazing. It may end at a well-known beauty spot. Possibly, a pick-up truck is waiting, or even a bridge to nowhere, or an old-folk's home with tartan carpets, or a strange wild building on top of a sea stack, demitting stone by stone into the waves far below. The road may end in Sabbath silence and wind, or nothing at all.

I left the memorial, got back on the bike and headed into town, ready to travel home. The students would be arriving at the university, expecting to learn how to deal with this mortal life in language, how to sculpt something beautiful out of silence. I'm not sure if I can help. Perhaps I'll take to speaking in riddles, like an oracle in a lonely cell. When they get stuck or overwhelmed,

I'll intone: "Let the muscles relax, the skeleton's doing the work." "Using no words, describe your ideal Sabbath." "Remember, the end of the road is also its beginning." "You are doing it," I'll reply.

"Your own room," my sister was saying. "Some of your own furniture."

"Company when you want it . . . ," I added.

"How's your mother?"

"She's doing okay."

"Peace and quiet when you don't."

Our grandmother was looking us, one to the other. Neither her grandchildren, nor her great-grandchildren have inherited her hazel eyes, more's the pity, or that long hawkish nose. She was beginning to nod in agreement.

"Meals all cooked, ay? No washing up."

"Someone to keep an eye on you."

"You wouldn't have to worry . . ."

My sister and I glanced at each other, and spoke both at once. "Move in myself," I muttered. She said, "Where do I sign?"

The school bus passed, and when its noise abated all I could hear was wind in the electric wires. A man in blue overalls was closing his gate, a collie at his feet. He watched solemnly as I cycled by.

Cetacean Disco

None of the crew were out of their twenties. Three Scots lads: James, Brennan and Hamish. Hamish led us — a silent group of eight, strangers to each other, but suffused with unspoken yearning — down pontoons to the boat. It was a glorious day in Tobermory. The sea sparkled, the sky was blue, the hills of Ardnamurchan and Sunart, across the water, seemed amazed by the light.

As we nosed out of the bay, James climbed barefoot up onto the viewing deck, and sat on the floor. He apologised for his visual aids: a file of pictures still soggy from yesterday's rain. He began telling us what we might look for, what we might see. Minke whales. Porpoises, for sure. Male orcas have long straight dorsal fins. Minkes are forty feet long, about the length of this boat. He told us the highlights, like the time they encountered a school of 150 common dolphins, or last year's sudden influx of orcas — killer whales. Minkes don't show their tail flukes when they dive. "If you see tail flukes," he grinned, "shout! And look for rafts of feeding birds. If they suddenly lift away, it could be because a whale's about to breach beneath them. But, you just never know. You never know what might turn up."

Might turn up, but probably won't.

Whale-watching, cetacean-watching proceeds like a kind of theology — by glimpses, sightings, a dorsal fin, a rolling back. A pursuit for the regretful; all might-have-beens and what-did-we-miss? You can buy a little field guide to fins.

As we rounded the point of the lighthouse, raft after raft of Manx shearwaters lifted from the water before us. A couple of gannets passed overhead. Then we were out at sea and heading straight toward a vast, rust-coloured container vessel, the *Ambassador,* as it steered into the Sound of Mull. Clinging onto the chrome rails, we thumped and bounced over its wake. The lads were sitting on the roof of the wheelhouse, eyes shaded against the glare. A century ago, these would have been the very men putting out with the whalers, out of Stromness and Stornoway, to get themselves locked up in the Arctic ice. Now, for a fee, they were showing the whales to us.

The boat pitched and rocked. The low islands of Coll and Tiree slumped across the southwestern horizon. North was Eigg, and the abrupt hills of Rhum, where storm petrels live. But all around us was water and, above, clear sky. Cloud was piled up over every heave of land. Over the water, however, the sky was bright, untroubled blue. In the salt wind and sunlight, you could feel your skin tighten. There was nothing but the sparkling sea, the islands, the too-bright sky. We were all quiet, watchful, until the woman beside me poked my shoulder and cried. "There!"

Two dorsal fins, travelling north, side by side.

"Those are Risso's dolphins!" Hamish called. "Good start!"

You get your eye in, quartering the sea, moving your gaze from the middle distance to middle-far, out of the dazzling band of sunlight spilling from the southwest. At first every wave seems a rolling back, every cormorant a fin, but —

"Minke whale! Two o'clock!"

What you see is a dense, black curve. Neither a wave nor an island. The whales rise and tip slowly, almost with a laze or languor. Everything else glitters, but among the glitter rises a thick black crescent. Usually the eye works the other way, ready to pick out a gleam in the dark. Today we were watching for a heave of blackness amongst all that light.

Six o'clock! Did you see it?

Another — four o'clock!

James made tea, brought it up the ladder in insulated plastic cups with slightly sentimental paintings of British wildlife. I got badgers, the women beside me jays.

Then the dolphins arrived, as you might say, out of the blue.

We were moving in wide zigzags, seeing what we could see, and then suddenly they were all about us, port and starboard, bow and stern, aligned with the boat and travelling at pace with us, leaping and diving. The lads were cock-a-hoop. James swayed with one hand pressed to his forehead — I don't know what they are! "They arenae common, arenae bottlenose. This is amazing!"

He rummaged through the Cetacean ID book, grinning.

"What do you think? That one or that one? We've never seen these before!"

"I think that one. That yellow bit on the flank . . ."

"I agree. Hamish?"

But Hamish, in the wheelhouse, was already on his mobile. "Hey, we've got forty white-sided dolphins out here! No, really!"

The propulsion of the boat pushes the water ahead of it into a clear, thick band, and that's where dolphins like to be. We were lying down, side by side, leaning out over the low deck so we looked straight down into the water. They'd come alongside, dark powerful streaks, vanish for a moment beneath the boat, then loom up directly in front of us, their outlines sharpening as they rose. When they breached, they were almost close enough to touch. With one fluid movement, they'd arch clear of the water, breathe, then the blowhole closed, the fin followed, and down they went.

"Babies! Oh, for god's sake, will you look at the babies!"

I don't know whether they always travel like this, the mothers with young at the centre, flanked by wingers and outriders, but in the bow-wave were two, three, such pairs — muscular adults with young striving alongside like small earnest shadows. We clapped and shouted, cheered when they leapt clear.

Then: "Whale! Lunging! Behind the dolphins! God almighty! Cetacean disco!

When we cut the engines, a great silence fell, like the silence of the beginning of the world. Then there were bird calls, and the gentle plashy sound of dolphins. Brennan, as skipper, cleared his throat, put on his professional voice. "As you may have realised, this is a first. . . ." But then he was laughing again: "Thirteen years — we've never seen white-sided dolphins. I mean, they exist but usually way out west in the Atlantic. Not around here."

Someone said, "All we need now is killer whales."

James said, "Damn. Brennan, did you mind and book the killer whales?"

But the mobile rang and Hamish answered. "That's them now. They're gigging in Stornoway. Gonna be ten minutes late."

For a while, we all travelled north together, dolphins and boatful of people. In the binoculars, I could see two small energetic wind turbines on the foreshore of Eigg. Behind, a little to the west, rose the hilly hulk of Rhum, Behind again, the hills of southern Skye. Then, abruptly, the dolphins peeled off northwest, and we watched them go, their dorsal fins rising and falling.

We watched until we could see them no more, and it was time to turn back to harbour. By then the sun was setting behind Tiree, flushing the cliffs of Ardnamurchan with calm light. The water was sheeny in the gloaming. We all sat quietly side by side at the front of the boat. A gleam reflected on the bow rail dazzled us all the way home.

KATHLEEN JAMIE was born in the west of Scotland in 1962. Her poetry collections include *The Tree House* (Picador, 2004), which won the Forward prize and the Scottish Book of the Year Award; *Jizzen* (Picador, 1999), which won the Geoffey Faber Memorial Award; and *Waterlight: Selected Poems* (Graywolf Press, 2007). *Mr & Mrs Scotland Are Dead* (2002) was short-listed for the International Griffin Poetry Prize, and in 2002 Jamie was awarded a Creative Scotland Award. A part-time lecturer in Creative Writing at St Andrews University, Kathleen Jamie lives with her family in Fife.

The text of *Findings* has been set in Warnock Pro, a typeface designed by Robert Slimbach for Adobe Systems in 2000. Book design by Wendy Holdman. Composition by Prism Publishing Center. Manufactured by Versa Press on acid-free paper.